THIS IS
SYDNEY

THIS IS
SYDNEY

TEXT BY WENDY MOORE

Published in Australia by
New Holland Publishers (Australia) Pty Ltd
Sydney • Auckland • London • Cape Town
14 Aquatic Drive Frenchs Forest NSW 2086 Australia
218 Lake Road Northcote Auckland New Zealand
24 Nutford Place London W1H 6DQ United Kingdom
80 McKenzie Street Cape Town 8001 South Africa

First published in 1996
Second edition published in 2000

National Library of Australia Cataloguing-in-Publication Data:

Moore, Wendy.
This is Sydney.

Includes index.
ISBN 1 86436 597 8.
ISBN 1 86436 639 7 (pbk.).
1. Sydney (N.S.W.)—Pictorial works. I. Title.

919.441

Publishing Manager: **Mariëlle Renssen**
Commissioning Editor: **Sally Bird**
Structural Editors: **Thea Grobbelaar and Joanne Holliman**
Internal design: **Lyndall Hamilton**
Cover design: **Nanette Backhouse**
Picture Researcher: **Vicki Hastrich**
Illustrator: **Richard Pooler**
Reproduction by cmyk prepress
Printed and bound in Singapore by Tien Wah Press (Pte) Ltd

Frontispiece: *Viewed from the harbour's northern foreshores, Sydney lights up against a spectacular sunset.*
Title page: *Visitors relax in the sun at First Fleet Park with a clear view of the Opera House across Sydney Cove.*
Page 7: *Milsons Point at the northern end of the Harbour Bridge provides a great vantage point to view
the festive Australia Day celebrations.*
Contents Page: *The Cruising Yacht Club marina in Rushcutters Bay clearly indicates Sydney's passion for sailing.*

Greater Sydney

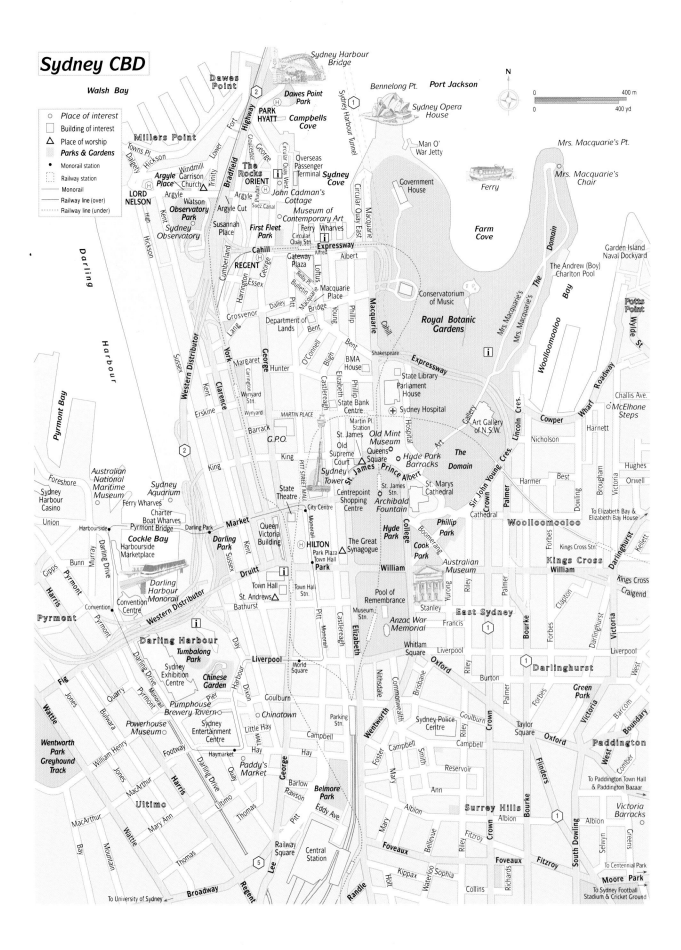

Sydney CBD

Legend

- ○ Place of interest
- □ Building of interest
- △ Place of worship
- ▓ Parks & Gardens
- • Monorail station
- ⬚ Railway station
- — Monorail
- — Railway line (over)
- ⋯ Railway line (under)

N

0 ——— 400 m
0 ——— 400 yd

Walsh Bay
Dawes Point
Millers Point
Darling Harbour
Pyrmont Bay
Pyrmont
Ultimo
Wentworth Park Greyhound Track

Sydney Harbour Bridge
Dawes Point Park
Campbells Cove
PARK HYATT
The Rocks
ORIENT
REGENT
Argyle Place
Garrison Church
LORD NELSON
Observatory Park
Sydney Observatory
Susannah Place
First Fleet Park
Overseas Passenger Terminal
Sydney Cove
John Cadman's Cottage
Museum of Contemporary Art
Ferry Wharves
Circular Quay Stn.
Cahill Expressway
Gateway Plaza
Macquarie Place
Department of Lands
BMA House
State Library
Parliament House
State Bank Centre
G.P.O.
MARTIN PLACE
Martin Pl. Station
Sydney Tower
Old Supreme Court
St. James
Queens Square
Old Mint Museum
Hyde Park Barracks
Sydney Aquarium
Charter Boat Wharves
Pyrmont Bridge
Cockle Bay
Harbourside Marketplace
Darling Park
State Theatre
Centrepoint Shopping Centre
City Centre
HILTON
Park Plaza
Town Hall
Queen Victoria Building
Town Hall Stn.
St. Andrews
The Great Synagogue
Hyde Park
Archibald Fountain
St. James Stn.
St. Marys Cathedral
The Domain
Phillip Park
Cook Park
Australian Museum
Darling Harbour
Tumbalong Park
Sydney Exhibition Centre
Chinese Garden
Pumphouse Brewery Tavern
Powerhouse Museum
Sydney Entertainment Centre
Convention Centre
Chinatown
World Square
Paddy's Market
Haymarket
Belmore Park
Railway Square
Central Station

Sydney Harbour Tunnel
Sydney Opera House
Bennelong Pt.
Port Jackson
Man O' War Jetty
Mrs. Macquarie's Pt.
Mrs. Macquarie's Chair
Ferry
Government House
Farm Cove
Conservatorium of Music
Royal Botanic Gardens
Garden Island Naval Dockyard
The Andrew (Boy) Charlton Pool
Woolloomooloo Bay
Potts Point
Wylde St.
Art Gallery of N.S.W.
Challis Ave.
McElhone Steps
Woolloomooloo
Kings Cross Stn.
Kings Cross
Pool of Remembrance
Anzac War Memorial
East Sydney
Sydney Police Centre
Taylor Square
Darlinghurst
Green Park
Paddington
Victoria Barracks
Surrey Hills
Moore Park

To University of Sydney
To Elizabeth Bay & Elizabeth Bay House
To Paddington Town Hall & Paddington Bazaar
To Centennial Park
To Sydney Football Stadium & Cricket Ground

Sydney Harbour Casino
Australian National Maritime Museum
Foreshore
Ferry Wharves

Broadway

Photographic Acknowledgments

Don Fuchs: p. 95; **Bill Green:** pp. 10, 26, 38, 48, 52 (bottom), 53 (bottom), 84 (top), 92, 98 (top); **GMP:** p. 13 (bottom); **Heidi Herbert:** p. 138 (bottom); **NHIL:** pp. 18 (top), 144; **NHIL** (Shaen Adey): back cover (middle), title page, pp. 7, 14 (bottom), 17, 23, 35, 36, 42, 52 (top), 60 (top), 64 (top), 65 (top right), 70, 71 (top right), 72 (top), 73 (top left, bottom), 77, 79 (centre right), 82 (bottom), 83 (top), 84 (bottom), 86, 87, 90, 91, 98 (bottom), 99 (top left), 100, 101, 102 (top right, bottom), 103 (bottom), 104 (top), 105 (bottom), 106, 110, 111, 113, 114, 115, 116/117, 119 (bottom), 120, 122, 123, 124/125, 126 (top right, bottom), 127, 132 (top left, top right), 133 (top), 134, 135 (bottom), 136 (bottom), 137 (bottom), 141, 142/143, 146, 154, 155; **NHIL** (Anthony Johnson): pp. 8/9, 13 (top), 18 (bottom), 22 (bottom), 24, 28, 29, 30, 33, 49, 53 (top), 54, 55, 56/57, 66, 68/69, 72 (bottom), 74/75, 76, 78 (top, bottom right), 79 (left), 80, 81, 82 (top), 83 (bottom), 88 (bottom right), 93 (top left), 94, 96, 107, 108, 112, 118, 121, 126 (top left), 130/131, 135 (top), 136 (top),139, 140; **NHIL** (Nick Rains): front cover, back cover (top and bottom), half-title page, pp. 15, 16, 21, 22 (top), 25, 31, 32, 34, 37, 39, 40, 41, 43, 44, 45, 46, 47, 50/51, 58, 59, 60 (bottom), 61, 62, 63, 64 (bottom left, bottom right), 65 (top left, bottom), 67, 71 (top left, bottom), 73 (top right), 78 (bottom left), 79 (top right, bottom), 85, 88 (top, bottom left), 89, 93 (top right, bottom), 97, 99 (top right, bottom left, bottom right), 102 (top left), 103 (top), 104 (bottom), 105 (top), 109, 119 (top left, top right), 128, 129, 132/133 (bottom), 145, 147, 148, 149, 150, 151, 152, 153, 156, 157; **NLA:** pp. 19, 20; **Nick Rains:** p. 12; **SLNSW:** pp. 14 (top), 27; **Susan Wright:** pp. 137 (top), 138 (top).

The following abbreviations have been used:
GMP Graham Monro Photography Pty Ltd
NHIL New Holland Image Library
NLA National Library of Australia
SLNSW State Library of New South Wales

Copyright is held by agents or photographers in **bold type**

CONTENTS

PROFILE OF SYDNEY
10

The Harbour 15
National Parks 17
Sydney's Wildlife 18
First Settlement 19
The Rocks: Cradle of Sydney 21
Georgian Beginnings 23
Royal Botanic Gardens 25
Modern Icons 26
Around the Harbour by Ferry 28
The Lively East 30
Architecture: From Victorian
to Art Deco 33
Beguiling Beaches 35
Heading West to Parramatta 38
The Blue Mountains 42
A Taste of Olde England 44
The South Coast 45
Central Coast & Hunter Valley 46

THE CITY AND THE HARBOUR
48

THE SUBURBS
96

OUTSIDE SYDNEY
144

INDEX
158

PROFILE OF SYDNEY

From a height of some 8 kilometres (5 miles), the passengers aboard a jumbo jet flying through a cloudless ultramarine sky look down over a vast striated plain, the ochre-coloured landscape that comprises the greater part of Australia. Hours later, the first road, like a line drawn with a ruler, appears; then sporadic homesteads are glimpsed, their postage-stamp tin roofs glinting in the sun and looking far too small to be the hub of cattle stations larger than some European countries. Later, the farms shrink, the rolling plains grow greener, and the plane begins to descend over the box canyons of the bush-cloaked Blue Mountains. Grids of suburbia finally appear. Red-roofed houses swathe the plains below and cluster more densely until, like the finale of a stage show, Sydney Harbour is revealed. The city sparkles in the sunshine by the jewel-like waterway, aptly dubbed 'the finest harbour in the world' by Sydney's founding father, Captain Arthur Phillip.

Sydney Harbour is a spectacular vista. The cobalt-blue water, across which arches the majestic steel span of the Harbour Bridge, is speckled with yachts; sunlight bounces off the gleaming sails of the Opera House; a cluster of glass and metal skyscrapers marks the central business district; and Victorian terrace

This aerial view of Sydney Harbour is a reflection of why Sydneysiders are so proud of their city and why it is Australia's major tourist destination.

houses, apartments and bungalows tumble down the hillsides to boat-filled bays and secluded sandy coves. On the banks of the upper harbour, a spectacular athletics complex with state-of-the-art stadiums is home to the 2000 Olympics. It is little wonder that Sydney lures 2 million international visitors each year and over 4 million local tourists.

Australia's firstborn city is still the most magnificent. Sydney is the New York of Australia. It is bigger, taller, brasher, livelier, and when the sun is shining, it is breathtakingly beautiful.

The majority of the first European arrivals were convicts transported to the other side of the world to ease the overcrowded prisons of England. But even when they had acquired their tickets of leave, most stayed on in the new land as wages were higher and there were boundless opportunities.

Sydney's story began on 26 January 1788 when a group of indigenous Aborigines watched in astonishment as a fleet of British ships anchored at a small cove. Strange white-skinned men stepped ashore and took possession, naming the place Sydney, after Thomas Townshend Sydney, the English public servant who had first mooted the idea of establishing a penal colony in the Antipodes. Very few of these first intrepid settlers could ever have imagined that just over two centuries later Sydney would boast almost 1000 suburbs encompassing an urban area six times that of Rome with a population of just over 3.7 million.

On a typically sunny summer afternoon, capacity audiences will turn out to watch the Australian cricket team compete in World Series matches at the Sydney Cricket Ground.

A Quixotic Climate

The novelist Patrick White, Sydneysider and Australia's only winner of the Nobel Prize for Literature, once wrote that Sydney was a 'compound of San Francisco and Chicago'. The former is self-explanatory, as both have world-renowned harbours, but comparisons with the latter probably have more to do with Chicago's energy and brashness than its geographical situation. However, Chicago's sobriquet, 'the windy city', could apply when the winter southerlies with their Antarctic bite blast through Sydney's inner-city canyons. But both cities of White's comparison are too far from the tropics. Sydney is considered to be quasi-tropical. Frangipanis and bougainvilleas thrive in the gardens, and rainforests of cabbage tree palms and native figs swathed with lianas still survive in secluded bush gullies.

When the British first set eyes on the Sydney landscape, they were stunned by its weirdness. These first immigrants tried to replicate the English landscape but were ultimately forced to accept their new environment and learn its secrets, like how native wildflowers bloom throughout the year and that the brightest displays are in winter when the wattles paint the bush a brilliant chrome yellow. But not only did the trees shed bark instead of leaves and

the animals hopped about instead of walking on all fours, the seasons also seemed topsy-turvy – winter fell in June and summer in December.

In summer the mean temperature hovers around 23°C (73°F) and in winter it is about 12°C (54°F). But statistics are deceptive. In practice, it is not so simple. Sydney weather is much more quixotic. The temperature can easily reach the summer mean on an August day in the middle of winter, when office workers shed their woollens and sunbake in Hyde Park at lunchtime. And when all of Sydney, it seems, has emptied onto the beach on a scorching summer day, a southerly 'buster' can suddenly blow up, sending beach umbrellas cartwheeling and the thermometer plummeting.

Away from the balmy influence of the harbour and the ocean, the climatic range is even greater. Far western suburbs like Richmond consistently record below-zero morning temperatures in winter, while in midsummer the 'westies', as the inhabitants of this region are affectionately known, regularly bake in temperatures of over 40°C, or over the ton (100° on the old Fahrenheit scale).

Life in Sydney is split by the dichotomy of its two main seasons, summer and winter. Summer is the beach: swimming, surfing, beer and barbecues. Summer is cricket: lazy days when test games can

have aficionados glued to the television for several days at a stretch. Winter is football – especially Rugby League, the Sydney-based game which dominates primetime television. Winter is also the bush, when hiking is best because the snakes are hibernating and devastating bushfires are unlikely.

Water has a moderating influence on the climate but more on the real estate market. Over 30 suburbs have the Pacific Ocean as their backyard. Scores more suburbs can claim an ocean view which adds thousands to the value of a home. According to the experts, 'position, position, position' are the three fundamentals for obtaining a good price, and position is all about water views, especially harbour views, and preferably those which include the Opera House and the Harbour Bridge. The city's highest priced real estate perches on the sandstone ledges and secluded coves surrounding the 55 square kilometres (21 square miles) of harbour. In ritzy Darling Point, a pocket-handkerchief-sized block of land would be worth millions, if you could find one.

Multicultural Sydney

For perhaps the first 150 years of Sydney's existence, the city suffered from a severe case of Anglomania. Not only did the majority of the population trace its roots back to the British Isles, but a couple of world wars, where Australian troops fought on Britain's behalf, consolidated the bond. In 1836, when Charles Darwin sailed into Sydney Harbour aboard the *Beagle* in the course of gathering information for his overhaul of the theory of humanity's origins, his 'first feeling was to congratulate [himself that he] was born an Englishman'. Not everyone, however, was of the same opinion, particularly the Irish who were already waging a centuries-old war against the British on their home soil. When they came to Australia, they continued their anti-authoritarian behaviour, and it was no coincidence that most of the best-known bushrangers of the colonial era were Irish by birth. In 1827, 'Bold Jack' Donohoe, the first bushranger to be romanticised by a ballad, escaped from a chain gang and held up

At the Harbourside Marketplace in Darling Harbour there are over 50 different international food outlets catering for the city's tourists and office workers.

a bullock dray on the Windsor Road. Only three years later he was killed by a hail of bullets while he cursed the troopers who caught him, but he had already cast the mould of the brazen larrikin who scorned the Establishment. This popular folk hero pervades Australian culture, and Paul Hogan capitalised on it with his portrayal of Crocodile Dundee. This film, the most successful ever made in Australia, crystallised this image of the archetypal Aussie, especially on the international scene where Australians had long been seen as essentially rural people. However, nothing could be further from the truth. Australians were in the past, and are today, overwhelmingly urbanites. In New South Wales alone, around three-quarters of the population live in Sydney, and a reasonable percentage of the remaining quarter lives in the other urban centres along the coastal fringe.

The typical native-born Sydneysider was first stereotyped in the 1820s when the Scottish naval surgeon Dr Peter Cunningham, who was the surgeon-superintendent on five convict transports, wrote that they resembled Americans. They were tall, lean, blue-eyed, fair-haired, big on mateship and going to the beach, and sexually forward. While this may have been a reasonable illustration of a fair percentage of Sydney's inhabitants until comparatively recently, the attitudinal switch in immigration policies after World War II inexorably changed the picture. Over a million of today's Sydneysiders were born overseas, and one in four come from non-English-speaking backgrounds.

Sydney has large established populations of Southern Europeans from Greece, Italy, Malta, Spain and the former Yugoslavia. There are Arabic-speaking peoples from the Middle East, predominantly Lebanese and Turkish. There are Chileans, Peruvians and Brazilians. There are Maoris from New Zealand, and Islanders from all over the Pacific; and there are the Kooris, as the indigenous Aborigines of the Sydney region prefer to be known. These fragment cultures have revitalised the city. These days Sydneysiders can pick and choose from a staggering array of takeaways, from Malaysian laksa and Japanese sushi to Mogul curries and Turkish shish kebab. The Vietnamese surname Nguyen is ousting longstanding favourites like Smith and Jones in the Sydney telephone directory, and Buddhism is the fastest-growing religion. Almost eight per cent of Sydneysiders were born in South-East or North-East Asia and Chinese is now the second most popular language next to English.

During the 19th-century gold rushes, thousands of Chinese people worked on the goldfields. However, relations between them and the white miners were exacerbated by the latter's Euro-centric cultural outlook. They accused the Chinese of sending the nation's wealth overseas, of immorality and all kinds of crimes, but the workers were most concerned about the diminishing gold reserves and were fearful that 'coloured' labour would lower their wages. It was really cultural and economic insecurity which prompted the Immigration Bill excluding immigrants because of their colour, so it appears that it was only when Australia was mature enough and confident of its own identity that it could open its gates to all peoples and become truly multicultural.

The largest single demographic change in the Sydney landscape came when Asian refugees and migrants were admitted after the scrapping of the controversial 'White Australia Policy' (the

Chinese Opera, originally staged for the enjoyment of emperors and deities in China, now entertains the audiences at the Chinese New Year celebrations held annually in Dixon Street, the heart of Sydney's Chinatown.

Arriving in their new homeland, a family of English migrants, lured by the promise of a sunny prosperous land, disembarks from the Empire Brent *in 1948.*

unofficial name of the government's restricted immigration policy) introduced in 1901 to keep out these same ethnic groups. Despite this, most Chinese miners returned home after the gold-rush days, but some stayed on to run market gardens in what are now the upmarket suburbs of Rose Bay, Roseville and Pymble. In 1910 when Sydney's markets opened at the Haymarket, many Chinese people moved into the area, bringing their laundries, cabinet-making businesses, restaurants and dry goods stores with them. Chinatown evolved around the narrow thoroughfare of Dixon Street which, about 80 years later, surrounded by streets of Asian restaurants and other businesses, and embellished with matching pagodas at either end, still serves as the traditional hub of Sydney's exploding Asian com-munity. These days most of the migrants from North-East Asia, including quite a sizeable percentage who have quit Hong Kong before the 1997 takeover, live in the inner west or on the North Shore,

while the majority of the South-East Asian arrivals, including rather a large community of Vietnamese refugees, live in Cabramatta, which has undergone the biggest cultural transformation of all Sydney's suburbs in the last decade. From a sleepy, outer-western suburb it has metamorphosed into an energetic Saigon streetscape. Cabramatta has both its detractors and its admirers, but one thing is for certain – this suburb is the face of Sydney's future.

Although Europeans of non-English-speaking background only migrated en masse after World War II when the Labor government offered assistance to refugees – some 170 000 arrived between 1947 and 1954 – it wasn't until 1969 that their cultures began to alter not only the culinary habits but also the attitudes of the average Sydneysider. After the British, the Italians were the second-largest group of migrants during the 1940s and 1950s. They settled in the inner west, partic ularly in the area around Leichhardt, where some pioneers had first estab-lished an Italian enclave just after World War I. People of Italian descent now live all over Sydney, but Leichhardt is still famous for the city's best Italian cakes and bread and for its Norton Street cafes where coffee aficionados still argue over the merits of Lavazza or Vittoria.

Nowadays, Sydneysiders are inclined to take for granted the huge array of fruits and vegetables that is available, but before the Sicilians and Calabrians began their market gardens at Penrith and Fairfield (now subdivided into housing estates) in the 1950s, few Aussies had heard of, let alone eaten, a capsicum or an eggplant, and tomato sauce was used only to douse their chops and sausages. These days, the pizzerias are the most prolific of all the eateries, and even the city's very few remaining staunch Anglophiles would no doubt know how to cook spaghetti bolognaise; such is the influence and proliferation of Italian cuisine.

Just as the Italians rejuvenated the city's green-groceries, so did the Greeks inject new vigour into the seafood scene when thousands of Greek migrants came to Australia on assisted passages in the years between 1953 and 1956. Like the other ethnic groups, a handful of pioneers established a pattern which the later settlers followed. In the 1870s, a couple from the island of Kythera opened a fish shop in Sydney; four decades later there were around 400 of their fellow islanders working in the city's seafood businesses, a trend which is still evident today, as most of the fish and chips shops are owned by families of Greek descent.

Named after its London namesake, the Covent Garden Hotel on the corner of Chinatown's Hay Street overlooks Paddy Market, established by the Chinese community in 1910.

In the late 1930s, after the German invasion of Austria and Czechoslovakia, many thousands of Jews who fled in order to escape Nazi persecution arrived in Sydney. The disproportionate percentage of intellectuals and professionals amongst this group of immigrants made an enormous impact on the city's artistic and academic scene, and was also largely responsible for the resulting cultural renaissance – the first real flowering of a much more cosmopolitan Sydney.

Political refugees have been arriving in Sydney since the city's earliest days, when a sizeable proportion of the Irish transported were convicts only because of their anti-British sentiments. Australia was, as the historian Robert Hughes aptly dubbed it, 'the official Siberia for Irish dissidents'. Hungarian refugees arrived in Sydney after the Russians crushed their nationalist revolt in 1956, then again 10 years later after the invasion of Prague. Refugees in flight from the civil war in Lebanon are the reason why approximately 80 per cent of Sydney's 100 000-strong Muslim community is of Lebanese descent. Left-wing Chileans arrived in Australia after the military takeover of their country, Salvadorans escaped from terror squads, and the most recent refugees include Bosnians in flight from the ethnic-cleansing campaigns of the Serbs.

Although roughly 75 per cent of the population is still of Anglo-Celtic origins, Sydneysiders lead the push for a republic, widely expected to coincide with the turn of the century. The great majority favour ousting the Queen as head of state, as allegiance to royalty is seen as important to only a small minority of conservatives. For most Sydneysiders, Asia rather than Europe is seen as the nation's future direction. Sydney was once regarded as being at the end of the world, but with the economic rise of the Asian-Pacific nations it is increasingly being perceived as being in the forefront of a new world order. As the head of the Olympic committee said when awarding Australia's premier city the right to host the 2000 Olympics, 'and the winner is – Sydney'.

Dobroyd Head offers spectacular views of the harbour entrance, and bushlands that are relatively unchanged since the area was occupied by the indigenous population.

THE HARBOUR

There are places around Sydney Harbour – in heathlands atop sculpted sandstone cliffs, on bushland trails which wind past forests of gnarled eucalypts, or even in secluded foreshore bays – where it is easy to imagine that the last 200 years of European settlement have been little more than a dream. Some of these pockets of primeval scenery, looking much the same as they have for thousands of years, are only a short distance from the centre of Australia's biggest city. But it is wrong to imagine that the bush is unchanging, as ever since the harbour was created it has been in a constant state of flux.

Archaeologists use carbon dating and other scientific methods to decipher prehistoric times, while Aboriginal Australians have their myths and legends which tell of how it all began back in the Dreamtime, the era when spirit ancestors shaped the land and created every living thing. These tales tell of volcanic eruptions, of times when the sea swamped the land and when the dry eucalypt forests were lush, tropical rainforests. Largely discounted in the past – like the Greek myth of Troy which has been proved to be a historical reality – many Aboriginal legends are now being scientifically substantiated. The time span of Aboriginal habitation in the Sydney area alone is currently estimated at about 40 000 years, but newer methods of carbon dating are constantly pushing back these figures. Dates are quite often outmoded as soon as they are published. However, it is hardly surprising that the indigenous myths tell of rising and falling sea levels, as 18 000 years ago when the world's oceans were glaciated by the ice age and water levels were about 100 metres (328 feet) lower than today, Sydney Harbour would have been a river valley. Later, as the climate warmed and the ice melted, the oceans rose until around 6000 years ago when they reached today's levels.

At Mount Wilson in the Blue Mountains, avenues of deciduous trees shade English-style holiday homes built last century by well-heeled Sydneysiders; but back in the mists of time this popular retreat was a volcano, and geologists are only now realising that the Aboriginal myth of an exploding mountain refers to the creation of Mount Wilson. Likewise, climatologists are in agreement with indigenous tales of lush rainforests in areas now typified by dry eucalypt forests, as the continent has become increasingly dry over the ages. In moist, protected gullies, remnants of primeval rainforests still survive, proof of the Aboriginal Dreamtime stories.

In early 1995, in a remote gully in the vast Wollemi National Park which stretches north-west from Sydney's outer fringes, botanists discovered an entirely new species of tree, which amazingly, although it is over 30 metres (98 feet) high, had never been glimpsed before. The Wollemi pine is a subtropical tree which was growing at the time when dinosaurs roamed, and in this remote gorge, accessible only to expert abseilers, the only known group of these trees in the world is found. The location of these trees is the botanical world's best-kept secret, understandably so since preservation, not extinction, is the key word today. However, this was not always the case, especially with regard to the indigenous Aborigines.

The Aborigines of the Harbour

In 1788, as the First Fleet made landfall at Botany Bay before moving north to what is now Sydney Harbour, Aborigines on the foreshore shouted 'Warra warra!' meaning 'go away', to the strangers disembarking on their shores. Lieutenant Philip Gidley King, in charge of one landing party, tried the old colonial ruse of appeasing the natives with beads and ribbons, but the Aborigines were more interested in finding out if the bizarre newcomers were in fact humans.

Change arrived with the newcomers; unfortunately, they were much more interested in imposing their own ideals than in learning what the Aborigines had to offer. This Eurocentric attitude was so deeply entrenched that the first white occupants of Sydney took little account of the vast array of native foodstuffs available to them and instead eked out a near-starvation existence on their paltry, maggot-riddled rations brought from England. Ironically, for the original inhabitants – the Cameragal, Wallumedegal and Booregegal of the northern shores, and the Kadigal of the southern coves – Sydney Harbour was the source of abundant foodstuffs and

Aboriginal Dreamtime legends inspired this wall mural adorning a Victorian terrace house in the inner-city suburb of Newtown.

resources. They took to the harbour in bark canoes, and suitably impressed Lieutenant William Bradley, namesake of the harbour's Bradleys Head, by their dexterity in heavy seas. On board the canoes, a fire was kept burning on a pat of wet clay or seaweed, and this was used for grilling fish, keeping warm and for light at night when fishing in quiet bays. The women fished using opalescent hooks carved from turban shells as lures, and the men speared fish, often while lying perfectly still across their canoes with their heads underwater for greater vision. Shellfish, particularly the Sydney rock oyster which is renowned by gourmets worldwide, was a favourite food source. Middens – ancient refuse mounds of thousands of discarded oyster, mussel and cockle shells bleached by the sun over time – are still found around Sydney, from the dunes of Barrenjoey Head in the north to the coves of Sydney Harbour National Park.

According to Aboriginal belief, Aborigines belong to the land and the land belongs to them, a symbiotic relationship which has existed since creation. Their ancestors journeyed across the land, sculpting the mountains, harbours, rivers and plains, and creating the plant life, birds, beasts and human

beings. Since then, all of these elements have been enmeshed in an intricate relationship with each other. If part of this balance is affected, the whole is affected, as conservationists now realise. The Aborigines were experts at keeping the balance in their environment. They knew to the day when the salmon were running, when the lilly pillies with their vitamin-rich berries were flowering and when the time was right for burning off the land – knowledge gleaned after millennia of continual occupation. Today, bushfires are started by pyromaniacs, lightning or discarded cigarette butts. For a Sydneysider, bushfires are just as much a symbol of the summer as the beach is, but much more dangerous. A hot north-westerly gale can blow a fire out of the bush and towards the city's suburbs in a few minutes. The worst bushfires in living memory occurred in the New Year of 1994. Fire surrounded the city, burning out scores of homes and causing fatalities. Before contact was made between Aborigines and Europeans, grasslands and forests were set alight by the locals in order to regenerate countless species which only germinate after extreme heat. Bushfires also provided the means to drive animals out into the open where they could be hunted. After the whites came, however, the land was never the same again.

Terra nullius means 'the empty land' in Latin and, despite the presence of occupants, the English claimed Sydney for the Crown using this phrase, because no one came forward to sign treaties. The Aborigines believed they had been the owners of their lands since their ancestors had created them. Now they were being driven out of their family territories, away from the sacred sites of their religion and culture, away from the shrubs, plants and animals that constituted their traditional foods and medicines, away from their world.

Captain Arthur Phillip, the founder of Sydney, was a man of the Enlightenment. In 18th-century fashion, he viewed the Aborigines in a more benevolent fashion than his antecedents did. He was under royal order to respect them and not to harm them. The official stand was equal rights for all – but unofficially all the rules were broken. This was the era of the 'noble savage', the time when indigenous peoples were looked on as being in an unpolluted state, like Adam and Eve before the Fall. Artists of the time pictured Aborigines in this manner: proud and tall, like Spartans on old Greek goblets. But when they didn't do what was expected of them, the official line changed. The Aboriginess had actually been waging guerrilla warfare over land rights ever since the English had landed, but to preserve the myth of the 'empty land', they were portrayed as aimless nomads. Nothing could be further from the truth, as everything they did was intimately connected to the management of the environment. But it was not farming as the British knew it, who were hungry for land to farm in the European manner. This meant that large expanses of grassland were needed to support imported grazing animals.

When Darwin's evolutionary theory put Australian Aborigines on the bottom rung of the ladder as the 'missing link', it conveniently worked in with colonial expansionist policies. Social dominance justified all, especially the land grab needed to expand the fledgling colony, and the official attitude hardened. The

government sought to turn them into farmers, but the Aborigines proved to be a problem. Resistance leader Pemulwuy waged a 12-year war against the British before he was killed by bounty hunters in 1802. The Sydney clans were driven further and further from their ancestral lands. A century later, decimated by alienation, culture shock, alcohol and introduced diseases, Australia's total Aboriginal population had shrunk to around 48 000, from a pre-European-contact number of which estimations vary from 300 000 to 1 million. Today there are 65 000 people of Aboriginal and Torres Strait Islander descent in New South Wales, around one-third of whom live in Sydney, mainly in the inner-city suburbs of Redfern and Matraville, and beside Botany Bay at La Perouse. Since the 1960s, Aboriginal people have made significant gains in their fight to regain their land and their culture, notably the landmark Mabo decision in 1992 which recognised pre-existing native ownership of the land.

Aboriginal people today are found in all walks of life, from law to the per-forming arts; and in direct proportion to their population size, Aboriginal sports stars dominate in rugby as well as track

and field. The works of indigenous artists are shown in Sydney's leading galleries and their characteristic style of painting has been duplicated on items in souvenir shops from Darling Harbour to Darwin. But so much of their art was lost, never to be found again. Perhaps the city's litany of Aboriginal place names is the only link between today's Sydneysiders and the earliest inhabitants of Sydney. Looming above the northern harbour entrance is North Head, a sandstone cliff sculpted by the Pacific breakers. The Aborigines aptly named it Boree, which means 'the enduring one', while Barrenjoey, the northernmost headland of Sydney's beaches, means 'a young kangaroo'. The name for Bondi Beach comes from the sound of the surf rolling in, while the name of the nearby beach of Coogee means 'rotten seaweed'. Wahroonga, on the elite North Shore, means 'our home' (which puts paid to the myth that the Aborigines didn't 'own' the land) and the name of Taronga Park Zoo is derived from 'a beautiful view', which is obvious to any visitor.

NATIONAL PARKS

More tangible remains of Sydney's first inhabitants are found in the bushland reserves surrounding the city. These contain vast tracts of countryside where protected native flora and fauna still survive, along with middens and rock engravings. On the southern outskirts of Sydney is Australia's oldest national park, the Royal National Park, gazetted in 1879. Within its 15 014 hectares (37 100 acres) is a range of ecosystems, from windswept heathlands to gloomy subtropical rainforests. The region was once home to the Dharawal people, whose hand stencils and rock engravings are still found here, as are their creek names like *burunda* for the black swan and *gorra warra* for the laughing jack-ass, also known as the kookaburra. In spring, the heathland is alive with flannel flowers, flaming bottlebrushes, vermilion Christmas bells, and statuesque Gymea lilies with a single monumental scarlet flower atop an alum spear. Lady Carrington Walk, where visitors can cycle

It is believed that the first Aborigines to arrive at Sydney Harbour made the trek 40 000 years ago, which makes European arrival, only 200 years ago, seem minute in comparison.

Koalas, named after the Aboriginal word for 'no water' because they seldom drink, once roamed Sydney's bushlands, but are now mainly found in wildlife sanctuaries.

or walk the 9.5-kilometre (6-mile) historic route along the Hacking River to its source, was named after a governor's wife when it was opened in 1886, promoted as 'the most beautiful drive in the world'. Sydney's high-profile and vocal conservation movement had its first major victory here in 1922 when this historic rainforest, once ruthlessly plundered for joinery and cabinet-making, was saved from the loggers.

Creeping up to the backyards of the city's northern suburbs and extending to Broken Bay, 20 kilometres (12 miles) further north, Ku-ring-gai Chase National Park offers a diverse range of scenery from rugged gorges to the secluded bays of Pittwater, the Hawkesbury River and Cowan Creek, which are favourites for weekend river cruises. Within the park are 180 Aboriginal rock-carving sites dating back 150 to 3000 years with life-size outlines of whales, sharks, stingrays, and half-human, half-animal figures which supposedly assisted in passing on the oral myths of Aboriginal culture and religion. For an insight into Aboriginal life in pre-European-contact days, take the Garigal Aboriginal Heritage Walk from West Head. The trail, named for the local dialect group, provides marvellous vistas of the drowned river valley of Broken Bay and of Lion Island, the haunt of fairy penguins and hawk's-bill turtles, through to heathlands ablaze with golden wattles in the winter and aromatic boronias and pink grevilleas in the spring. There are Aboriginal carvings, middens and caves with ceilings blackened over the centuries by the Garigals' cooking fires. Plants used by the indigenous people are signposted: the spiky shafts of *xanthorrhoea* were used for spears, while the resin from the

trunk was used as a glue in weapon- and tool-making. The knobbly growths on the red gums were fashioned into water vessels, while the lacquered orange seeds of the spiky burrawang palms – relics from the dinosaur age – were ground into a flour for making damper (native bread).

Sydney's latest gazetted park, Sydney Harbour National Park, is also the closest to the city centre. Visitors merely have to catch a ferry to Taronga Park Zoo for a two-hour walk around the harbour foreshores to Clifton Gardens, or alight at Manly for the 10-kilometre (6-mile) walk to Spit Bridge which takes in forested gullies, beaches, bushland and Aboriginal sites.

SYDNEY'S WILDLIFE

When the first European botanists came upon the native flora and fauna of Sydney, they were stupefied. Europeans didn't know what to make of kangaroos and wallabies which hopped rather than ran on all fours, or of koalas that resembled bears but were nocturnal marsupials unrelated to any known species, past or present. The platypus was even more perplexing: what to make of a creature with fur like a seal, a tail like a beaver, webbed feet and a bill like a duck, and which not only laid eggs but suckled its young?

The koala is without a doubt the animal mascot of Sydney. Koala motifs adorn everything from souvenir mugs to designer T-shirts. They are so irresistibly 'cute' that in Japan they are as popular as rock stars. When the 1994 bushfires swept through much of Sydney's bushland, the Japanese raised a substantial fund for the rehabilitation of the koalas. Most of Sydney's koalas, though, like the larger mammals of the region, moved out to safer, less-populated environments decades ago. At Taronga Park Zoo, koalas clamber down from their perches to munch on fresh eucalypt leaves – their only food – while cameras and videos click and whirr. Koala Park Sanctuary at West Pennant Hills attracts thousands of visitors, and patting and posing with the koalas is the major drawcard. Feeding kangaroos is another

Even the elephants at Taronga Park Zoo enjoy the view. The zoo has been consistently voted the world's most spectacular and is only 12 minutes from Circular Quay by ferry.

popular pastime for visitors, especially at Waratah Park adjacent to the Ku-ring-gai Chase National Park, where the internationally renowned television series *Skippy* was filmed.

Even the birds are quite extraordinarily different from those in Europe, especially the brilliantly coloured parrots and cockatoos, such as the rainbow lorikeets with their blue heads, bright green tails, tangerine breasts and orange and yellow underwings, and the grey and pink galahs which appear to change from one colour to the other as they fly. The birds can be quite cheeky too. A flock of squawking rosellas can strip a ripe fruit tree within minutes, and if a blue peg disappears off a clothes line, it has probably been pinched by a satin bowerbird which decorates its 'bower' or mating area only with blue objects. The sharp crack of a whipbird echoes from many a bushland gully, and towards evening the manic cackling of kookaburras echoes over the treetops. Sometimes it seems as if the bush is alive with the sounds of birdsong. But for sheer audio power, nothing beats the cicadas: insects which fill the summer air with a racket that far exceeds the acceptable limit for noise pollution and is said to top even the decibels emitted by jet aircraft take-offs over Sydney's inner-west suburbs.

The city also has other even more notorious creatures. The deadly Sydney funnel-web spider is known to crawl up through the plumbing into the bathrooms of some of the most elite suburbs; but for sheer terror, nothing beats those dreaded denizens of the deep – sharks. Bronze whalers, responsible for a number of shark attacks in the past, have been known to venture upriver right to the freshwater line, making the deep inlets of Sydney Harbour unsafe for swimming unless the beach is netted. However, there hasn't been a fatality for decades, as all of the city's main surfing beaches are now netted. These days sharks are protected, especially the snout-nosed Port Jackson shark which spends most of its days lying at the bottom of the harbour waters. This harmless shark is indeed a creature of the earliest Dreamtime, as fossils of this family date back 200 million years.

FIRST SETTLEMENT

One of the greatest riddles of maritime history is why such a renowned navigator as Captain James Cook, the first known European to discover Australia's east coast, considered Botany Bay an ideal site for the continent's first settlement when the superior Sydney Harbour lay only 20 kilometres (12 miles) to the north. After spending a week in the bay, which he named after the amazing variety of botany it displayed, he wrote in his diary: 'Having seen everything this place afforded we put to sea.' With no offence intended to Botany Bay's inhabitants, Cook's parting remark could well be true today. With its entrance fringed by oil refineries, its bay cleft by the international airport runway, and pseudo-Mediterranean villas lining its shores, the bay's sights hardly compare with those of its famous sister to the north which, surprisingly, Cook sailed past after prosaically noting that 'there apper'd to be a safe anchorage which I call'd Port Jackson'.

On the basis of the week spent at Botany Bay, Cook informed his superiors that it was an ideal site for a settlement as the bay was deep enough for sailing vessels and the soil was good. Eighteen years later when Captain Arthur Phillip sailed into the bay at the head of a fleet of 11 ships carrying nearly 800 convicts, he was stunned to discover how wrong Cook had been. The soil was sandy, the waters were shallow, and there was no fresh water, let alone the 'fine meadows' the great navigator had enthused about. Of course, no one had ever checked Cook's report, as no ships visited the area between 1770 and 1788. The east coast of Australia was about as remote from European civilisation as it could be. Two centuries ago, most of the world's surface was unmapped by Europeans; the poles, and the interiors of Africa, the Americas and Asia were all *terra incognita*.

There were several reasons why Britain decided to establish a penal colony so far from its own shores. Cities and towns had expanded with industrialisation, London's population had doubled between 1750 and 1770, and the gulf between rich and poor was enormous. The privileged classes considered the lower classes a threat, especially after the French Revolution, and draconian punishments were imposed for trivial crimes. British gaols were so crowded that convicts had been transported to America, but after the American War of Independence closed

This early etching depicting Captain Cook's arrival at Botany Bay in 1770 shows alarmed Aborigines threatening the newcomers with spears.

Convict Joseph Lycett's 1825 engraving of Sydney Harbour seen from South Head shows the original inhabitants in the foreground.

this exit, British administrators began to look in earnest towards their latest acquisition, Cook's Botany Bay.

The First Fleet's eight-month, 24 000-kilometre (14 914-mile) journey was more like an epic adventure. In order to pick up the best currents and winds, the voyagers sailed across the Atlantic to Rio de Janeiro, then back to Cape Town, and then across the loneliest stretch of all, the Indian and Southern Oceans, where they laboured up the mountainous swells and plunged down into the troughs until finally the fleet sailed into Botany Bay.

Captain Arthur Phillip gave up on Botany Bay after two days and sailed north to look for a more suitable site for a settlement. He was on his way to Broken Bay, which Cook had also praised, when he entered Port Jackson merely for a look. Needless to say, after gazing upon what he considered the world's best harbour, there was no need to venture further north. After deciding on a deepwater cove watered by a small creek which he named Sydney, in honour of Thomas Townshend, 1st Viscount Sydney – the administrator who had argued in favour of transportation – he founded the settlement on 26 January. This date is now known as Australia Day and honoured by a public holiday as the birth of a nation.

Few tangible remains survive from the city's earliest days, but the basic street layout from Circular Quay to Town Hall, especially George Street (the oldest thoroughfare in Australia), the green lungs of the city such as the Botanic Gardens and Hyde Park, and even the quarter-acre block which characterises suburbia today, were all devised by Phillip.

Not much thought had been given to how the settlement was to look after itself, but then very little had been known about their destination. The fleet resembled a veritable Noah's ark. Animals of all description, numbering 500 in all, as well as plants and seeds, from coffee to oranges, had been taken aboard for this grandiose colonial experiment. When they first sailed up the harbour, they compared the well-spaced forests on the foreshores to an English deer park. The lack of undergrowth was due to Aboriginal 'firestick farming', where the bush was set alight to regenerate itself and attract game. Unsuited to the climate, early gardens like those at Farm Cove, where the Royal Botanic Gardens now thrive, were a failure. The dense hardwoods with their twisted trunks were useless for ships' masts.

The majority of the early settlement were convicts who marched down Sydney's streets in their leg chains, dressed in homespun cloth daubed with arrows (there were only 25 free settlers by 1800). Most of them had never been out of their native counties, so the surrounding bush must have seemed as 'funereal' as the melancholic writer Marcus Clarke described it, with stifling 'black gorges' inhabited by savages and 'grotesque or ghostly' animals. But this did not deter many of the convicts, who saw the bush as the only alternative to a life in chains, especially the Irish who had already waged a war against the British in their own land. So little was known about the interior that when a rumour circulated that only a river separated Australia from China, dozens of Irish prisoners bolted for the bush, only to die of starvation or to be recaptured.

Some convicts defied the odds, though, and became successful in their own right. At the age of 13, Mary Haycock was transported for horse-stealing. Four years later she married the ship-owning merchant Thomas Reibey and bore him seven children. When he died in 1811, she expanded his business and eventually owned a fleet of trading ships, several farms and a swathe of city real estate. Her grandson later became premier of Tasmania, and her warehouses still survive in Reiby Place in The Rocks. Samuel Terry, an illiterate thief, was another success story: on attaining his freedom he became a moneylender and publican, and ever mindful of his roots, the 'Rothschild of Botany Bay' never flogged the convicts who laboured on his 8000 hectares (19 768 acres).

In all, over 160 000 convicts were transported to Australia from that first fateful day in 1788 until the middle of the 19th century. Living conditions on the early square-riggers were horrendous, but after the surgeon William Redfern, whose name lives on in an inner-city suburb, made far-reaching changes, the death rate fell from around one in four on the worst ships to one in a hundred. However, it was still an ordeal which had an overwhelming influence on all those who had shared in it, especially as the majority of the crimes were petty offences often committed in poverty-stricken desperation. For instance, a 70-year-old man received seven years' transportation for stealing a block of cheese, while an 11-year-old boy received the same sentence for pilfering a pair of stockings and some ribbon. Out of this era was born the culture of mateship and the anti-authoritarianism that for so many years symbolised what it was to be an Australian male. At a recent royal commission into police corruption, it was shown that sticking by your mate, even if he is corrupt, is an essential ethos. In the same way, convict ancestry is not something that Sydneysiders keep as a skeleton in the closet; it is a background that carries considerable weight in the highest echelons of the city's social life.

THE ROCKS: CRADLE OF SYDNEY

Circular Quay is Sydney's tourist hub and is conveniently situated halfway along the waterfront promenade which joins the city's best-known icons, the Harbour Bridge and the Opera House. Only a few blocks west is The Rocks, the nation's oldest urban settlement, a maze of heritage pubs, outdoor cafes, restaurants, art and craft galleries and historic buildings. Behind the Quay tower the office blocks of the central business district, while to the east are architectural gems of the Georgian and Victorian eras, and the famed Royal Botanic Gardens. Circular Quay's greatest attraction, however, is its ferry terminal. Here teenage boys wearing outsize clothing, baseball caps on backwards and elongated backpacks containing their bodyboards (small surfboards) swarm onto the Manly ferry fired up with anticipation of a day to be spent riding the Pacific breakers. Video-camera-toting Japanese tourists at Wharf 5 board the boat for the souvenir shops of Darling Harbour, while the members of a large family lug their picnic baskets aboard the ferry bound

Campbell Cove was once a notorious seamen's haunt but is now home to the luxury hotel, the Park Hyatt; restaurants and galleries have now moved into the heritage buildings.

for Taronga Park Zoo. It has been two centuries since Captain Phillip founded the city here, and Sydney Cove is still the heart of the metropolis.

In February 1995, an archaeological survey revealed that the foundations of the historic buildings of a battery, built in 1791 when Britain was at war with Spain, and its guardhouse and officers' quarters lay buried beneath the lawns of Dawes Point Park. Although this scene is reminiscent of digs undertaken a long time ago at remote locations, barely a dozen metres away are the massive granite pylons of the Sydney Harbour Bridge, while the site is shadowed overhead by the immense steel carriageway of the Bradfield Highway with its incessant traffic. Ever since construction of the bridge began in 1925 and the historic buildings of Dawes Point in The Rocks area of Sydney were demolished, it had been assumed that the battery had also been totally destroyed. This is only the latest of several important archaeological finds in The Rocks, as this sandstone promontory on the western shore of Sydney Cove has witnessed every chapter of the city's past. But The Rocks is much more than just a well-restored 19th-century

enclave, as this popular tourist venue is also renowned for its galleries, restaurants, waterfront cafes, pubs and cultural events. As The Rocks' best-known entrepreneurial restaurateur, Neil Perry, said, 'This area is the lounge room of Sydney.'

Named after the 46-metre-high (151-foot) rocky ridge on which the settlement was built, The Rocks today is gentrified with superbly restored Georgian townhouses, converted sandstone warehouses and some of Sydney's most elegant hotels, all sympathetically built to merge with the 19th-century landscape. But it was not always so elite. From the very beginning, The Rocks was known as one of the bawdiest, raunchiest quarters of the Pacific, and as a notorious thieves' kitchen.

First Fleet Park, named after Captain Arthur Phillip's disembarkation point on the west side of Circular Quay, was where all the male convicts were landed and is a fitting place to begin a tour of this historic pocket of Sydney. At bustling Circular Quay, ferries arrive and depart, their ferry screws churning the deep-green waters of Sydney Cove into veined marble. Passengers board the beamy green-and-yellow *Freshwater* bound for Manly, while the sleek River-Cat takes off upriver for Parramatta. Meanwhile, a trio of Canadian sailors come ashore from the frigate *Vancouver*, docked at the Overseas Passenger Terminal – a reminder that The Rocks still has a link with its maritime past.

Facing Circular Quay, across Alfred Street, is the former Customs House, a magnificent Victorian edifice which houses Australia's largest collection of indigenous arts and craft.

Beside First Fleet Park is the Museum of Contemporary Art, the city's latest contribution to its burgeoning arts scene, which is housed in the former Maritime Services Board building, a superb sandstone edifice in late Art Deco style. Nearby is the city's oldest house, a tiny Georgian cottage which looks as though it was transplanted from the Irish countryside. Cadman's Cottage, built in 1815 and now housing the National Parks and Wildlife Office, was named after John Cadman, an ex-convict who was pardoned and became the superintendent of government boats. In those days, before land reclamation widened the foreshore, the waters of Sydney Cove actually lapped at the back door of the cottage.

Old stone steps, worn into the bedrock by two centuries of pedestrians, lead up to the northern end of George Street, the main thoroughfare of The Rocks. This street once housed the brothels and all-night taverns which gave the area its well-deserved reputation. The Orient Hotel, curving around the corner of Argyle Street, could well have been where drunken sailors were slipped Mickey Finns and shanghaied by corrupt publicans in league with ships' captains desperate for a crew, especially during the gold rushes of the 1850s when sailors deserted their posts in droves and the wharves were clogged with crewless square-riggers.

Hogarthian bedlam is how The Rocks was portrayed in histories of the time: harlots caroused in the streets and booze flowed freely at around 50 taverns. Historians have always recorded Sydney's earliest days as being particularly rum-soaked, although recent scholars are beginning to doubt that it was as bad as previously pictured. However, there is no exaggerating the importance of this potent liquor during the first decades of white settlement, and the effect that it had on the creation

of Sydney's psyche. The New South Wales Corps, nicknamed the Rum Corps for their monopoly of the colony's favoured beverage, effectively ran Sydney after Captain Phillip's departure, reversing many of his more democratic policies. They even used government money to fund the officers' personal purchases, such as entire shipments of rum which they then resold at enormous profit. Rum founded the fortunes of many of the colony's *nouveaux riches*, and proceeds were even used to build the first hospital, still known as the Rum Hospital, which is now Sydney Hospital.

During The Rocks' less than salubrious heyday, the alleyways were rife with pickpockets and the cobblestoned lanes were awash with sewerage and crawling with rats. In 1900, after 100 deaths occurred following an outbreak of bubonic plague, many of the waterfront hovels were torn down and replaced. Suez Canal, the more delicate term for Sewers' Canal, is now home to craft galleries and restaurants, and it is hard to believe that public hangings once took place on the corner of Essex and Harrington streets, now the site of the luxurious Regent Hotel.

Whalers, sealers and clippers from all over the known world once docked at Circular Quay West, where the nearby old warehouses of Campbells Cove with their sawtooth roofs and sandstone walls have now been converted into galleries,

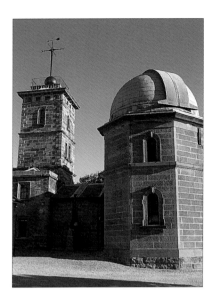

Sydney Observatory features a tower with a time-ball which drops daily at 13:00.

shops, and waterfront restaurants renowned for their seafood platters and alfresco dining. Like a ghost from the past, a schooner graces the docks, while a Baltic trading ship bobs at anchor and hoists sail every evening for a harbour dinner cruise. Wrapped unobtrusively around the wharf-front, the Park Hyatt Hotel, designed in Georgian sandstone style, affords its high-paying clientele a view to match the tariff: a sweeping vista of Sydney Cove with its glittering backdrop of steel and glass towers, and a cameo of the Opera House framed between the date palms in front of the hotel on Dawes Point.

The Rocks has undergone many facelifts during its chequered history, but the biggest upheaval occurred when the Harbour Bridge was being built in the 1920s and three entire streets were removed. The bridge and the connecting expressways now effectively cut The Rocks in two, but even in the past, when there was no such tangible barrier, there was an enormous gulf between the bottom and top halves of the settlement: the gentry lived on top of the hill and on the west of the promontory, while the riffraff, as the working class were known, resided on the steep eastern side around the wharves. As history generally recounts the lives of

Flanked by popular outdoor restaurants, Campbell Cove's warehouses, built between 1842 and 1861, are a historic reminder of The Rocks' heyday as a maritime entrepot.

the rich and famous, and their houses are usually the first to be preserved, it is a pleasant surprise to come across Susannah Place, a modest brick and sandstone terrace of four houses and a corner shop which has been continuously occupied by working-class families for the last century and a half. At 58–64 Gloucester Street, Susannah Place affords a rare insight into the lives of some average Rocks inhabitants.

A little further up Gloucester Street, burrowing under the expressway and connecting the two sides of The Rocks, is the Argyle Cut. This gloomy tunnel was painstakingly chiselled out of the cliff-face by convict labour. Work began in 1843, but was only finished 18 years later with the help of gunpowder. Larrikin gangs, the Aussie equivalent of hooligans, preyed on passers-by who were foolish enough to venture here after dark. Now part of the well-trodden heritage trail, the Argyle Cut has long outgrown its sordid past.

On the other side of the cutting is Sydney's only surviving 'village green' which has remained intact with its surrounding streets and buildings since its creation by Governor Macquarie in 1810. Named after his birthplace in Scotland, the square – Argyle Place – is flanked by elegant Georgian townhouses and is fronted by the Garrison Church (1840), named after the red-coated militia who marched here for prayers every Sunday. Providing the social balance, at the far end of the square is one of the city's oldest pubs, The Lord Nelson.

The best way to appreciate The Rocks and its strategic harbourside situation is to wander up nearby Watson Road to where the old Sydney Observatory crowns the hill. A veneer of verdigris coats the copper domes of these Florentine Renaissance-style buildings which served as the city's observatory from 1858 until 1982. It is now open to the public, and interested stargazers can still book night viewings. From the octagonal grandstand on the green knoll of Observatory Hill (previously known as Windmill Hill and Flagstaff Hill, for obvious reasons), undoubtedly one of Sydney's prime chunks of real estate, the circular vista is magnificent. From

Darling Harbour and up the Parramatta River, the glittery tentacles of Sydney Harbour extend to the west. Below, the windows of the Walsh Bay finger wharves flash like mirrors in the afternoon sun, while a catamaran leaves a spume of spray as it cruises under the bridge, heading towards the Quay where it will let down its passengers. The air is suddenly filled with the guffawing calls of a pair of raucous kookaburras which alight on a coral tree daubed with red blooms. It almost seems as if they are laughing at a secret joke. The Rocks has seen all kinds of changes in its two centuries of existence, but the kookaburras are oblivious to all this and remain as evidence of what this rocky promontory was like before the coming of the Europeans, when the Bidgigal people fished and gathered oysters around these shores.

GEORGIAN BEGINNINGS

Sandstone ledges, pitted and sculpted by the elements and scoured by ancient seas, wrap around the northerly tip of the harbourside garden known as the Domain. At the very end, on Mrs Macquarie's Point, one of the rocky slabs has been hewn into a seat. Legend has it that the promontory's namesake was often to be found here knitting sweaters for her husband, the governor, and between-time gazing at the view. Ever since, this hand-hewn seat has been known as Mrs Macquarie's Chair. The wonderful view, which juxtaposes the city's two leading icons – the Opera House and the Harbour Bridge – is a favourite photographic backdrop for wedding couples and tourists alike. Even though her talents were eclipsed by those of her famous husband, Lachlan

Macquarie, who transformed Sydney from a squalid penal settlement into a stylish colony, Elizabeth played a major role in bringing to fruition many of her husband's plans and schemes. During Macquarie's term of office, from 1810 to 1821 – the longest of all the colonial governors – the shoddy town underwent its first major urban renewal.

Governor Macquarie envisaged Sydney as a Georgian city in the mould of Edinburgh or Dublin, with elegant public buildings, townhouses, squares, villas and gardens complementing each other in a harmonious whole. In order for the governor to be able to embark on his urban renewal, considerable finance was needed. But London was not interested in improving the appearance or the social conditions of their penal colony. Instructions were to build only military and penal establishments. Macquarie had been given the job of steering the colony back to order after the chaotic 1808 rebellion by the Rum Corps against Governor William Bligh. He went ahead with his urban renewal, however, regardless of what his superiors thought; and like a true man of the Enlightenment era, he believed in the emancipation of convicts. Unlike his predecessors who had ruthlessly exploited their labour, Macquarie met every

Mrs Macquarie's Chair was fashioned from a sandstone ledge at the tip of the promontory which bears her name.

transport ship and personally instructed the internees on their rights. He was passionate not only about the transformation of the colony's features, but also about the quality of its life.

The Colonial Office in London was not about to send Macquarie an architect, so he found one himself. Francis Greenway had trained under John Nash, the pre-eminent architect of the day, but he had the misfortune to become bankrupt and, when caught for forging a contract, he was sentenced to 14 years' transportation. As an emancipated convict, Greenway was a perfect choice for the position of colonial architect; he was living proof of Macquarie's belief in the potential inherent in all of his prisoners. By utilising this pool of human labour (80 per cent of all convicts were used on government works), not only was Sydney redesigned, but with the colony's rapid expansion Parramatta and the Hawkesbury Valley towns were laid out, and roadworks radiated from the city to all points of the compass.

Macquarie Street, which boasts more historic public buildings than any other Australian thoroughfare, is the obvious place to begin a tour of 19th-century Sydney. If you start three blocks west at Macquarie Place, in the middle of a tiny triangular park shadowed by high-rise towers is a sandstone obelisk designed by Greenway, marking the spot from which all the colony's roads were measured. Continue up Bridge Street, passing the Lands Department Building, built between 1877 and 1890 in Classical Revival style, where famous explorers and bureaucrats are immortalised in stone. On the left-hand side is the old Treasury Building (1849) and Premier's Office (1894), which now form part of a luxury hotel. On the corner of Phillip Steet is the Museum of Sydney, built over the ruins of Governor Phillip's original 18th-century Government House which can be viewed through a perspex floor. The Chief Secretary's Building (c. 1878) brings a Parisian effect to this end of Macquarie Street as James Barnet, the architect, was heavily influenced by French Empire style. Opposite are the Royal Botanic Gardens, giving the street an ambience reminiscent of the thoroughfares which front New York's Central Park and London's Hyde Park.

Architecture buffs will appreciate the Art Deco BMA House, one of Sydney's first skyscrapers, which is decorated with medical and Australian symbols, including the koala. Home to the Australian Medical Association since 1929, this building was one of many which housed the city's most prominent doctors, as to be a 'Macquarie Street surgeon' was the highest accolade in the business.

Across the street, its massive colonnaded portico and sandstone walls bespattered with pigeon droppings, is the State Library of New South Wales, better known as 'the Mitchell' in honour of David Scott Mitchell, its greatest benefactor. Entrance is through copper doors embossed with bas-reliefs of famous explorers' heads, and underfoot is a marvellous mosaic of terrazzo, marble and brass, which recreates an intriguing early map of Australia by the Dutch navigator Abel Tasman. The east coast was as yet undiscovered, so its coastline is unfinished, while Tasmania is joined to the mainland; all around the continent are blue-striped oceans with galleons streaking across them in full sail. Inside the enormous main reading room, surrounded by tiers of books – part of the initial 1906 Mitchell bequest of 61 000 books and manuscripts – scholars and book-lovers sit at leather-topped desks and peruse their tomes under an enormous skylight which bathes the room in natural light. The only concessions to modern times are the computers and the quiet hum of the airconditioner.

The Mitchell Library is part of the State Library of New South Wales, which started in 1826 as a small subscription library and today houses over 3 million books.

The top section of Macquarie Street is where Parliament House stands, originally built by Macquarie as part of the Rum Hospital in 1816. In 1829 the first meeting of New South Wales' old legislative council was held and the state has been run from this Georgian building ever since. Florence Nightingale is said to have sanctioned the design of the nurses' quarters next door at the Sydney Hospital, built in 1894 in high Victorian style. Part of the old Rum Hospital still survives in the adjacent edifice which became the colony's Royal Mint in 1853. Today it houses a museum of Australian coins and stamps.

Queen's Square, at the very top of Macquarie Street and presided over by a statue of Queen Victoria, is the location of the most famous buildings of the Macquarie era, built by Francis Greenway. Standing back from the square is the imposing rectangular Hyde Park Barracks, built between 1817 and 1819. The clock framed by a pediment on the gable is Australia's oldest, and the interior has been painstakingly restored to portray how the 800 convicts who once lived here went about their daily lives. At the Barracks Cafe, visitors can sip their cappuccinos in what were once the original dormitories, the upper level being the cells where recalcitrant prisoners were held. The other two important Greenway buildings which once formed a pivotal part of Macquarie's urban renewal are the elegant St James Church, built in 1820 with a square tower and a copper spire, and the Old Supreme Court Building, Australia's second-oldest courthouse, which despite later additions still retains the understated Georgian elegance which is a hallmark of all Greenway's designs. Ironically, these very buildings, which are now lovingly conserved and widely appreciated, led to the fall of both Governor Macquarie and his colonial architect. The British authorities objected to the high cost of his public buildings, and the self-styled upper class of early Sydney railed against the governor's habit of giving trusted positions to ex-convicts. Like many creative souls, Greenway was ahead of his time. After Macquarie left the colony in 1821, Greenway had few job offers and died a pauper. But both men left an indelible impression on the urban landscape of Sydney and gave the city a sense of style which survives today.

ROYAL BOTANIC GARDENS

High up in the canopy of an enormous weeping lilly pilly, dozens of bats dangle like so many coat-hangers. These nocturnal fruit-feeders are quiet now that morning has arrived and almost look like part of the tree itself, until they rearrange their wings to make a kind of shade and the sunlight beams through the translucent, parchment-like skin. Beneath this century-old tree, fan palms and tree ferns quiver in the understorey, while on the forest floor few plants can survive in the shade of such a giant tree, a noticeable feature of all rainforests. However, this is not an average rain-

forest but part of the Royal Botanic Gardens, only a few minutes' walk from downtown Sydney.

Covering over 30 hectares (74 acres), this green oasis in the city centre showcases an enormous collection of Australian and exotic flora in one of the world's most stunning settings. The Gardens curve around the shores of Farm Cove, extending from the Opera House on Bennelong Point in the northwest, to Mrs Macquarie's Point at the eastern tip of Farm Cove. The western border is delineated by historic Macquarie Street, while the adjacent parklands, known as the Domain, border to the east and to the south, although the ill-conceived Cahill Expressway slashes through what was once an unbroken stretch of green.

The Royal Botanic Gardens, universally known as 'the Gardens', were originally Australia's first farm. Captain Arthur Phillip sent a party of his First Fleet convicts around to the next bay east from Sydney Cove to clear the land for agriculture – hence the name of the bay, Farm Cove. Corn was sown, but it was unsuccessful, although remnants of those first furrows are said to form part of what are now the prolific flowerbeds of the Middle Garden. After the original farm failed to produce – probably due more to the first farmers' misunderstanding of the climate than to the

quality of the soil – agriculture moved further afield to the newly discovered alluvial flats of the Parramatta River.

Governor Phillip was far-sighted enough to put aside not only what now comprises the Gardens, but also the adjoining Domain (once known as the Governor's Domain) and Hyde Park. But it was Governor Macquarie who officially designated the parklands as the Botanic Gardens in 1816. The crenellated stables and servants' quarters of Government House, which survive as the Conservatorium of Music, are remembered as the best-known architectural folly of Macquarie's chief architect, Francis Greenway. The Garden Palace Gates on Macquarie Street are a fitting entrance to one of the world's oldest and most renowned botanic gardens. This Art Nouveau entrance was built in 1879 by the Victorian architect James Barnet to complement the Garden Palace, a glass exhibition hall built for the International Exhibition of the same year. Tragically, only three years later it was destroyed by fire along with nearly all of Australia's most valuable Aboriginal and colonial artefacts.

In the Southern Hemisphere spring, from September to November, the Gardens are famed for their Azalea Walk when these colourful flowering shrubs explode in a riot of pinks and purples. In winter, the Camellia Garden is at its

The 180-year-old Royal Botanic Gardens, one of the world's leading botanic gardens, provides an oasis of tranquillity and greenery in the hub of the city.

best, as are many varieties of native flora including kangaroo-paws, grevilleas and the spectacular Gymea lily. Whatever time of year, it is always summer in the hothouse atmosphere of the Tropical Centre which specialises in rainforest plants from around the world. There are free tours on offer, but most visitors prefer just to wander around and discover the Gardens on their own.

All visitors to the Gardens are eventually drawn to the waterfront. Other international parks can boast greater botanical wonders, but none can rival the Gardens' harbourside setting.

A curving path follows the stone sea-wall around horseshoe-shaped Farm Cove, while ferries and yachts crisscross the waters behind the glinting wings of the Opera House. Behind Macquarie Street, the jagged skyline of geometric office blocks is topped by the soaring spire of Sydney Tower. On a rise overlooking the harbour vista, visitors exit the Gardens through the sandstone pillars of the Woolloomooloo Gates and cross the bridge over the Cahill Expressway to the adjoining parklands of the Domain. In the early days, entry to the Governor's Domain was restricted to the upper echelons of society. However, by the 1840s the rules had been relaxed considerably and the parklands were a favourite venue for

domestic servants on their day off. This was the beginning of the Domain's social-isation. By the 20th century, soapbox speakers were haranguing the crowds on everything from doomsday to communism and the need for an Australian republic. In the 1960s, 'flower-power' hippies dropped LSD at the Domain, and eccentrics like Bea Miles gave impromptu Shakespeare recitals. These days most people merely pass through en route to its greatest attraction – the Art Gallery of New South Wales.

On the solid sandstone walls are inscribed the names of famous artists, such as Michelangelo and Da Vinci, as well as others now known only to a handful of art historians. Built in 1909 by the colonial architect W. L. Vernon, the art gallery boasts a Classical Greek portico with impressive fluted columns. Australia's best-known painters are on display, together with an impressive permanent collection of Aboriginal and Torres Strait Islander artworks and touring world-class exhibitions. Like most of its clientele, the Gallery Restaurant is understated chic – all glass and chrome – and everyone is trans-fixed by the view outside the plate-glass walls. Boulder-like sculptures provide the foreground to a backdrop of pastel-coloured terrace houses which tumble down Woolloomooloo Bay to the blue

harbour. It is easy to see why Sydney's most famous artists have always been so enamoured of its water views.

MODERN ICONS

One of Sydney's favourite sons is the actor-cum-director Paul Hogan, better known on the international scene as 'Crocodile Dundee' for his successful parody of the 'ocker', the down-to-earth, matey Aussie bloke who is equally adept at foiling New York muggers as rescuing his leading lady from the gaping jaws of a crocodile in the outback. 'Hoges', as Aussies call him, moulded his on-stage persona not, as may be supposed, through many years spent working in the bush, but from his work mates when he was a painter on the Sydney Harbour Bridge. Those early days spent working on the city's best-known symbol certainly contributed to his iconographic stature. While Hoges nowadays spends his time in Hollywood, his ex-colleagues can still be seen scraping and painting on the great arch which, together with the Opera House, symbolises the quintessential Sydney.

If you look up to the top of the bridge from either side, you can see the painters silhouetted against the sky. They make it look deceptively simple,

In 1932 when the Sydney Harbour Bridge opened, its 503-metre-long (1650-foot) steel span, which attains a height of approximately 134 metres (440 feet), was the largest steel arch in the world.

especially when viewed from ground level, but it is no easy task to work 134 metres (440 feet) above sea level, even if the view is among the world's best. A unique new tour now takes visitors across the top of the arch, and while they wear special suits and harnesses, it is not for the faint-hearted.

It is as difficult to imagine Sydney without the Harbour Bridge as it is to picture Paris without the Eiffel Tower or New York without the Statue of Liberty.

Despite the fact that 150 years of European settlement passed before a bridge between the north and south shores of the harbour became a reality, the idea had been thrown around since the city's earliest days. During the early 19th-century building boom of the Macquarie era, the architect Francis Greenway proposed a bridge, as even in those early days settlers were beginning to populate the northern shores of the harbour. But the Colonial Office was already horrified at the new colony's building expenses, and turned down the proposal. Other plans met the same fate. A floating bridge was proposed, as well as a high-level bridge, a suspension bridge and a tunnel. Finally, a high-level bridge was declared the winner. Tenders were called for, designs were submitted, and then, in what was to set the scene for later large public projects, the government changed, leading to more bureaucratic inquiries and innumerable setbacks. In 1912, embarrassed into finding a solution, the government called on the chief railway engineer, Dr J. J. C. Bradfield, who submitted three designs including a cantilevered arch. Eventually, after being blocked for 10 years by various government bodies and unavoidable hitches such as the steel shortages of World War I, the proposal was passed in 1922. Tenders were called for once more and the winner was Dorman Long, an English engineering company.

The original estimate of 4 million pounds was considered an outrageous cost – it ultimately blew out to over twice that amount – but the state premier, Jack Lang, argued that the cost was necessary if the bridge was to handle the city's traffic 50 years into the future. As it turned out, the post-war economic boom and the mass production of the Holden, 'Australia's own car', which by 1960 had turned out a million vehicles, ensured that the bridge was already experiencing traffic jams a good couple of decades before Jack Lang's prediction. It took until the 1990s for a second link to be built when the Harbour Tunnel finally opened for business, but even this has done little to ease the city's traffic congestion.

Described as the 'engineering wonder of the age', the Harbour Bridge was a remarkable achievement, particularly when one considers that most of Sydney's traffic during the 1920s was horse-drawn. Custom-built steamships were constructed in Newcastle to bring 42 000 tonnes of granite for the pylons from Moruya, about 300 kilometres (186 miles) south of Sydney. Tunnels were hacked out of the harbour's bedrock for the foundation blocks and the great steel anchor cables that had to take the weight of the arches before they met in the middle. Cavernous workshops were erected in Lavender Bay to the west of the northern pylon where the steel spans were prefabricated and then hoisted up by cranes onto the arch. As the two arches gradually crept out across the harbour, Sydneysiders speculated as to whether they would actually meet, and it was indeed a delicate operation as they edged closer and closer. The cables were then loosened. When there were only a few inches to go, everything depended on the weather. Two dozen thermometers were placed at strategic points to warn the engineers if the temperature rose too high, as this could cause the metal to expand and jeopardise the final link. Finally, in the winter of 1930, to the relief of the engineers, the workers and the Sydney populace who

In 1930 Sam Hood, a Sydney photographer, hung precariously from the incomplete northern arch of the Harbour Bridge during its construction to capture this revealing photograph.

had been watching its progress over the last six years, the two arches were finally joined. Two years later the dual carriageway and the rail and tram tracks were completed, and just to dispel any fears that the 65 000-tonne span may have been inadequate for the job, 96 steam locomotives and two dozen coal tenders were driven onto the bridge. The contractors hailed the bridge as a British engineering triumph, but there were very few Sydneysiders who saw it as anything less than the first great Aussie achievement, a watershed marking the beginning of a new Australia freed from the colonial cultural cringe.

On 19 March 1932 the bridge was officially opened, but in what has become almost a tradition, the vital moment was marred by controversy. Just as Jack Lang, the premier of New South Wales, was about to cut the ribbon, a uniformed horseman charged forward and slashed the ribbon with his sword, declaring that he was opening the bridge 'in the name of the decent and respectable citizens of New South Wales'. Captain Francis de Groot, an ex-army officer and member of the right-wing New Guard who opposed Lang's socialist policies, was wrestled to the ground. The ribbon was rejoined, and as the premier snipped it in two, thousands of onlookers applauded, ferries and

En route to Manly, the Narrabeen, named after one of Sydney's northern beaches, passes Admiralty House atop Kirribilli Point. The house, which is the Sydney residence of the governor general, was completed in 1845.

tugboats hooted, the air force flew overhead and the Sydney populace swarmed across the roadway. The Sydney Harbour Bridge has been the city's most dominant symbol ever since.

Sydney's claim that it is Australia's premier city is certainly justified by its ownership of not one but two major icons – the Harbour Bridge and the Opera House.

'A stroke of genius' is what Edmund Capon, the director of the New South Wales Art Gallery, once called the Opera House, and there are few who would disagree. It stands alone in international architecture as an original. With its curved white roofs like spinnakers billowing in the wind, the Opera House looks more like a sculpture than a building. Joern Utzon, the brilliant Danish architect of what has rightly been called one of the world's greatest 20th-century buildings, is popularly thought to have been inspired by yachts on the harbour. The inspiration was, in fact, an orange cut into quarters. However, Utzon's creation now symbolises the city's love affair with sailing boats, aptly illustrated on any weekend when the water is packed with wind-powered craft.

It seems unbelievable today that such an audacious design could have been chosen by the judging panel, considering the style of buildings which were being constructed in 1957, the year Utzon's Opera House won the competition. The second- and third-placed designs with their blocklike halls and right-angle reliance were light-years away from the winning entry, one of 216 entries from 36 countries. It was a courageous and far-sighted decision, particularly in light of the monumental problems which arose during the construction of the Opera House. It was apparent early on that Utzon's initial costing of A$7.5 million was an underestimate, to say the very least. While the engineers tried to grapple with how to construct such a roof – particularly because they had no precursor to look to – and while the bureaucrats argued and the future tenants squabbled, costs began to skyrocket. The Opera House Lottery was established to help foot the bill, and with a winning booty of A$100 000, it wasn't difficult to persuade Sydneysiders to part with their money for a chance at the big one, given that the city has one of the highest percentages of gamblers in the world.

Utzon weathered the storm for almost a decade, but the final straw came when the state government changed hands in 1966 and the Conservatives returned to power. The architect was blamed for the cost blow-out (the final figure was A$100 million, about 13 times the initial quote) and the premier demoted him to design consultant. Sydney's arts scene was appalled. Over 1000 architects and artists took to the streets, a sculptor went on a hunger strike, and Sydney University distributed replicas of a letter from Michelangelo complaining about similar bureaucratic difficulties he had experienced while painting the Sistine Chapel. Utzon returned to Denmark amidst the controversy and a team of Sydney architects was brought in to complete the job. It was incredibly lucky that at least the exterior was completed by its creator, as it is quite apparent that the interior is inferior in design. Utzon later said, 'You cannot make a piece of art and let somebody else finish it'; but despite the prodigious problems and pitfalls, the Opera House is indeed a work of art.

Australia's most celebrated building opened in 1973 to such international acclaim that the controversies that had dogged it from its inception were almost forgotten overnight as Sydneysiders basked in the adulation. Finally, the Opera House opened for business, and over two decades later it is still the undisputed hub of Sydney's sophisticated music scene as well as being among the city's top tourist attractions.

AROUND THE HARBOUR BY FERRY

Creeping through Sydney's surbubs like the tentacles of a giant octopus are 55 square kilometres (21 square miles) of waterways, much of which can be explored by ferry. From the Circular Quay terminal, sleek RiverCats, named after Olympic gold-medallists such as swimmer Dawn Fraser make the western run up Parramatta River via Homebush

Bay, the site of the 2000 Olympics. Chunky, old-fashioned ferries zigzag across the harbour to leafy enclaves like Mosman and Cremorne in the north, to Rose Bay in the south and Hunters Hill in the west. Animal lovers can take the ferry to Taronga Park Zoo, where bush-walkers can alight to explore part of the Sydney Harbour National Park. Seafood enthusiasts head for Watsons Bay on the southern shores, history buffs can explore the heritage buildings of old Balmain, and the entertainment complex of Darling Harbour is but a short ferry ride from downtown. The possibilities are endless. Even if a tourist took only the suggested itineraries in the public transport booklet, a minimum of 12 days on the harbour would be required. This may seem excessive, but it must be stressed that a ride on a Sydney ferry is absolutely *de rigueur*: ferries are to Sydney what the gondola is to Venice or the cable car to San Francisco. To forego the experience is to miss out on the city's heartbeat.

From Sydney's infancy, settlement spread along the waterways. Roads and rail only came much later. The rough bush tracks which made overland travel an arduous affair were avoided if there was a navigable waterway. The best farmlands were along the western bays and rivers and in 1789, only a year after the colony was founded, the first ferry was launched. Hailed by a prominent advocate as 'the first triumph of local shipbuilders', *The Rose Bay Packet*, powered by sails (or oars if there was no wind), was given a less flattering nick-name by the convicts who rowed her: they called her 'The Lump'. Four decades later the first steam ferry, the *Surprise*, took to the water and lived up to her name on her maiden voyage to Parramatta by grounding on a sandbar and arriving eight hours late, by which time the welcoming crowds had given up and gone home.

Despite all the setbacks, though, Sydney Harbour's ferries were here to stay. Land agents even started up ser-vices to their new estates to persuade buyers, and a regular ferry was sufficient incentive for development.

Of all the harbour destinations, Manly –

fronting the Pacific Ocean and backing up to a sheltered northern cove – has always been the most popular. Named after its 'manly-looking' Aborigines by Sydney's founding father, Captain Arthur Phillip, this natural holiday mecca is renowned for its pine-fringed surfing beaches, funfairs, sidewalk cafes, pubs, restaurants and its livewire atmosphere. In the earliest days, getting to Manly was a tricky proposition if you didn't go by boat. Seven nautical miles turned into 60 miles (97 kilometres) by bush track. No wonder the ferry service proved so popular from its inception.

The first traditional Manly ferry, with its double-ended design, white funnels capped with black and its dark green hull, was the aptly named *Phantom*. She inspired many a legend, including the 'Hot Potato Club', which was formed when a bored passenger during one of the innumerable breakdowns thought of using the time to roast a potato in the firebox. Whenever the boat's boiler flooded, the captain would raise the sail and use this alternative power to get into port. In the old days the journey was just as exciting as the destination, and even though breakdowns are unlikely nowadays, the journey itself is still one of the main reasons for taking a harbour ferry ride.

As the ferry pulls out from Circular Quay, the Opera House is on one side and the Harbour Bridge looms overhead on the other, making it hard to know which way to look. The bridge is at its most awesome when viewed from water level, especially on the way to Milsons Point where the ferry berths virtually underneath the northern pylon.

The Royal Botanic Gardens in Farm Cove green the southern foreshores east of the Opera House, while on the north-ern point at Kirribilli are two mid-19th-century mansions, Admiralty House, where the governor-general puts up when in town, and Kirribilli House where the prime minister does likewise. Crowned by a Martello tower, Fort Denison comes into view. Dominating the tiny island, known as Pinchgut to early convicts because of its insufficient rations, the fort was built to house the most notorious of Sydney's prisoners.

On the northern shores, framed by high-rise apartments and sheltering the navy's submarine base, is Neutral Bay, where foreign ships were moored in the colonial days to prevent them from having a clear gunsight to Sydney Cove. Picnickers and walkers disembark at adjacent Cremorne Point for a scenic stroll around the foreshores with spec-tacular unimpeded panoramas of the city and harbour. The ferry heads east, past Mosman Bay, where secluded man-sions and plush apartments overlook the former whaling cove, and around to Little Sirius Cove where a century ago the renowned artists Tom Roberts and Arthur Streeton set up their artists' camp. They were the first painters to capture the unique colour and lumin-osity of the Australian landscape. Roberts and Streeton were city boys who liked to escape to the bush on weekends, just like their modern-day counterparts who still come to this secluded cove to find a retreat from the bustling city. On the hill above is Taronga Park Zoo, which is aptly billed as the zoo with the world's best view.

On the southern shores are the pro-montories and bays of Sydney's most expensive and exclusive addresses. Rushcutters Bay, where in the old days

A high-speed JetCat ferry leaving Circular Quay for Manly passes the Art Deco-style Museum of Contemporary Art.

two convicts who were collecting roofing materials were felled by Aboriginal spears, is now a parking lot for yachts and cruisers, the toys of the rich and famous who reside in the surrounding apartment towers, *faux* Mediterranean villas and elegant sandstone mansions. Property prices in adjacent Darling Point, Double Bay, Point Piper and Rose Bay are among Australia's highest.

As the ferry rounds Bradleys Head, the cliff-top lighthouse is a reminder of the perilous rocks at its base where Sydney's two worst ferry disasters occurred. In 1927 the *Greycliffe* was run over by the steamship *Tahiti* and 42 passengers were drowned, and later, in 1938, 19 people were killed when most of the passengers on the upper deck of the *Rodney* rushed to one side of the boat to get a better look at an American warship and caused the ferry to roll over and sink.

While practically every square metre of the southern shores is given over to luxury real estate, much of the northern side, now part of Sydney Harbour National Park, is still virgin bushland and there are trails which run for kilometres through the cliff-top heathlands all the way to Manly Cove.

The most exciting part of any ferry ride to Manly has to be when Middle Head is cleared and one first glimpses the Heads, the north and south cliffs that guard the threshold of Sydney Harbour. On most days you can feel the change from the calm waters of the inner harbour as the heavy Pacific swells roll through the opening. The highlight of many a Sydneysider's childhood was a ferry ride when a big sea was running. Sometimes you weren't allowed on deck because waves could wash over it. Even today, if conditions become too hazardous, the ferries are stopped. Old-timers tell of the time when the *Dee Why* breasted a huge swell and the piano took off across the top deck and smashed through the sides, ending up at the bottom of the harbour.

When the ferry at last clears the Heads and enters North Harbour, the swells abate as it makes its home run into Manly Cove. The passengers swarm ashore to spend a relaxing day at the beach, or just to eat fish and chips while walking along the pedestrian mall of the Corso before heading back on the ferry again. For many Sydneysiders, the journey itself is the best experience.

When the Sydney Harbour Bridge was built, linking the North Shore with the south, pessimists thought the ferries' days were numbered, but nowadays the ferries are just as popular as they ever were. When the Parramatta River ferry service was reopened after a multi-million-dollar operation to deepen the river, the service couldn't keep up with the demand. It seemed that everyone wanted to forego their cars in favour of the ferry, an understandable situation given the only alternative of driving along the traffic-clogged Western Distributor. When the state government wanted to reduce the number of ferries in the 1970s, a 'Save the Ferries' committee was formed and the backlash from the ferry-lovers was so vehement that the government proposing the cutbacks lost the next election.

Sydneysiders have an emotional attachment to their ferries which is wonderfully illustrated by an old-timer's reminiscence in Graeme Andrews' *Ferries of Sydney*. He tells the story of how a man in the 1930s was advised by his doctor to take a long sea journey for the good of his health. 'He bought a season ticket on the Manly ferry and travelled all day everyday.'

THE LIVELY EAST

The unlikely combination of being one of the nation's most populated areas, its most expensive real estate, one of the world's most perfectly preserved Victorian suburbs, its undisputed capital of sleaze, the largest gay enclave in the Southern Hemisphere, and having more art galleries and sidewalk cafes per square kilometre than anywhere else in Australia makes Sydney's Eastern Suburbs an exhilarating area for both residents and visitors.

The unofficial border which delineates where the city proper ends and the Eastern Suburbs begin is Whitlam Square at the beginning of Oxford Street, and everywhere east of Hyde Park and the Domain. It has always been an area of extremes. Woollahra, Vaucluse and the elite harbourside suburbs were always where the moneyed classes lived, whereas virtually next-door in Woolloomooloo, families lived in slums in Dickensian squalor. Paddington was formerly a ritzy, planned suburb, but fell into neglect when Sydneysiders forsook the inner city for the endless quarter-acre blocks of the outer suburbs. But in the 1960s it was rediscovered, and now the inner east, revamped and lovingly restored, is experiencing a new boom as some Sydneysiders desert the outer suburbs for a more exciting lifestyle closer to the city's hub.

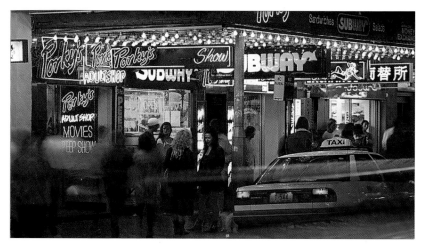

Darlinghurst Road in the centre of Kings Cross, Sydney's night-life hub, is flanked by night-clubs, strip-tease joints, fast-food outlets and X-rated video shops.

Taylor Square, straddling Oxford Street in the centre of Darlinghurst, is the pivot of the inner east and the capital of the gay scene, which has transformed this formerly derelict corner of the city into a cosmopolitan hub of cafes, restaurants, clubs and bookshops. Some boutiques specialising in 'S & M' leather gear and X-rated magazines have a limited appeal, as do some of the obviously anti-hetero pubs, but there is no denying the positive effect the gay scene has had on the wonderful array of eateries that proliferate along Oxford Street and its surrounds. Conservatives decry it, and Christian fundamentalists see it as a decadent omen, but the annual Gay Mardi Gras – a spectacle of kitsch and unadulterated hedonism held on Oxford Street – not only draws enormous crowds but, much to the dismay of its detractors, millions in tourist dollars.

Darlinghurst Road heads north from Oxford Street, bisects William Street (renowned for its daily metamorphosis from car showrooms by day to prostitutes' haunts by night), and burrows into the heart of Kings Cross, Sydney's notorious capital of sleaze. In the bright light of day it is hard to believe that this leafy grid of streets lined with Art Deco apartment buildings, flower stalls and coffee shops could warrant such a description, but after dark it is another story. The Cross, as most Sydneysiders know it, started life in the mid-19th century as a gentrified residential enclave, but its rough and tough image began to emerge in the 1920s when razor gangs, armed with cut-throat razors, robbed residents naive enough to wander the streets after dark. After an influx of poets, writers and artists who had fled the horrors of Europe during World War II, The Cross reinvented itself as the city's bohemian hub. Coffee shops hosted poetry readings, and bearded patrons discussed existentialism to the strains of classical guitars. Then came the Vietnam War, and as Sydney was the preferred destination for American servicemen on 'rest and recreation' leave, The Cross was reinvented once again. Discos, strip joints, American-style bars, marijuana and heroin were introduced in the 1960s, and it became Australia's official

Around the leafy side lanes of Kings Cross, a densely populated district, many small hotels now cater exclusively for backpackers.

vice capital. In the 1970s and even into the 1980s, a visit to Les Girls, famed for its drag queens, or to one of the many nightclubs was an essential part of a visitor's Sydney itinerary. These days it is sleaze with a capital 'S', complete with teenage prostitutes, homeless youths, drug addicts, 'shooting galleries' (rooms rented by the half-hour to heroin users) and X-rated book and video stores.

However, The Cross is not all bad news, as its thousands of residents and the international backpackers who flock there for cheap lodgings will attest, and a daytime stroll around the area uncovers some pleasant surprises. On Onslow Avenue is Elizabeth Bay House, a former colonial secretary's mansion dating from 1839. It has been restored and furnished in the Georgian style and features a wonderful staircase which winds up into a central domed saloon. Along leafy Victoria Street, many charming terrace houses and a few Georgian mansions are the proud survivors of the residents' bitterly fought campaign in the 1970s when, backed by the unions, they successfully resisted the government's plans to demolish their homes. At the Potts Point end of Victoria Street, the McElhone Steps lead down the sand-

stone escarpment to Woolloomooloo Bay. Opposite the finger wharf on Cowper Wharf Road is Harry's Cafe de Wheels, an all-night pie wagon frequented by generations of hungry revellers. The original wagon now resides in the Powerhouse Museum in Ultimo.

Differing theories abound as to the meaning of the obviously Aboriginal name, Woolloomooloo. Some historians suggest that it was how 'windmill' was pronounced, others that it meant 'whirling', but the most believable notion is that it is derived from *wullaoomullah*, which means 'young kangaroo' in the local dialect. Like Victoria Street, this district barely escaped being totally destroyed in the 1970s, but it still contains many picturesque old terraces and cottages which, like all the dwellings in the inner-east area, are being snapped up by the upwardly mobile.

From 'The Loo', head south on Bourke Street back to Taylor Square and east along Oxford Street to Paddington, the most unique of all the terrace-house suburbs built in the Victorian era. It seems unbelievable today that Paddington's original turn-of-the-century homes, some of Sydney's most sought-after residences, were only a couple of decades ago in danger of being demolished. There are few urban vistas as delightful as Paddington's tiered hillside, full of pastel-coloured houses which seem to march in rows down to the harbour. And there are few architectural vistas as stunning as the terrace houses along Liverpool Street, with their bullnose verandahs, fanciful iron lace, symmetrical chimneys, and facades of olive, cream, beige and ivory.

'Paddo', like most of the inner east, has experienced a roller-coaster of fortunes. In the early colonial days, the suburb was carved up into large estates with grandiose mansions such as 'Juniper Hall', built in 1824 and named after the principal ingredient for gin distilling, which secured the fortunes of the resident Cooper family. The patriarch, known as 'Robert the Large', apparently because of both his girth and philanthropy, was originally transported for smuggling, but after securing a pardon and a sizeable land grant for his distillery – a sure moneymaker – he went on to fame and fortune and sired 23 children. In 1984, his home, which is Australia's oldest surviving Georgian villa, was discovered behind a row of shops on Oxford Street and restored to its former glory by the National Trust. It now houses a private business.

In the 1880s, the original land grants were divided into housing estates and Paddington as it stands today was created. The crowning glory of Paddo's creation is its Town Hall on Oxford Street, surmounted by a 33-metre-high (108-foot) clock tower and built in Classic Revival style to celebrate the suburb's prestigious status. Ironically, though, by the time it was built in 1891, the terrace house was out of favour and Sydneysiders were flocking to the new garden suburbs. Paddo declined into a slum and only revived in the 1960s.

Also on Oxford Street, behind an imposing sandstone wall, is Victoria Barracks, a complex of military buildings which have been in constant use since their construction in 1841. These include a 220-metre-long (720-foot) regimental barracks which once housed 800 men, a guardhouse complete with punishment cells, and enormous native

fig trees and cabbage tree palms, the fronds of which were used by the soldiers' wives to weave hats. A few of the old sandstone cottages, where the tradesmen who built the barracks lived, still survive on nearby Gipps Street, as does a 1940s-style grocery store run by a couple of old Italian widows dressed in black who call their customers 'love' and 'darling'. With its wax-papered shelves and linoleum floor, the store and its proprietors are a touch of old Paddo, a remnant from the postwar days when migrants from the Mediterranean moved into the district, thereby saving it from the demolisher's hammer. A quaint reminder of the past, the store is surrounded by gentrified terrace homes, trendy cafes, and galleries specialising in rare books, handprinted fabrics, antiques and Persian carpets.

On Paddington Hill, clustered around the Uniting Church, Sydney's most popular village bazaar is held, boasting over 250 stalls which stock everything from handcrafted jewellery to original evening gowns by talented designers from the nearby Sydney Art School. Everyone flocks here on Saturdays, including some of the city's most bizarre characters, and even if you aren't interested in buying, the markets are a great place for people-watching and soaking up Paddo's unique ambience.

At the very top end of Paddington is Centennial Park, 220 hectares (544 acres) of gardens, bushlands, lakes and lawns popular with picnickers, joggers, birdwatchers, horse riders and cyclists. A pavilion marks the spot where Australia became a federation in 1901. Around the fringes of this vast green lung are some of the city's greatest sporting venues, including Randwick Racecourse, which is at its best during the Spring Racing Carnival; the Sydney Cricket Ground, where summer crowds gather to watch the Aussies take on the West Indies as well as other ex-colonial cricket nations; and the Football Stadium, shaped like a giant clam, where the rugby league grand final – Sydney's greatest sporting event – is hosted every winter.

Strung like pendants from the necklace of New South Head Road are the bays and promontories of the plush harbourside Eastern Suburbs. To the east of Kings Cross, and thrusting from the far side of Rushcutters Bay, lies exclusive Darling Point, home to the Gothic-style St Mark's Church where high society and occasional pop stars such as Elton John have recited their nuptial vows. Overlooking magnificent harbour vistas in streets lined with great shady camphor laurels, luxury apartments rub shoulders with grandiose

Paddington Bazaar, held each Saturday in the grounds of the Uniting Church on Oxford Street, features hundreds of different stalls and attracts thousands of visitors.

mansions such as 'Bishopscourt', home to Sydney's Anglican archbishop, which was originally built in the 1950s for Thomas Sutcliffe Mort who consolidated his fortune by initiating frozen meat shipments to Europe. Nearby is the 42-roomed mock castle known as 'Swifts', built by the brewer Robert Lucas Tooth in 1876. Another brewer, Edmond Resch, bought it in 1900, and in 1963 the family handed the residence over to the Catholic Church for the archbishop's seat, but it is now again in private hands. On the street of the same name is the Neo-Gothic 'Lindesay', believed to be the very first of the grand mansions of Darling Point. Built in 1843 for a former state treasurer, the residence has now been restored by the National Trust.

Double Bay – often referred to as 'Double Pay', which is evident to anyone scanning the price tags in its designer boutiques, the menus in its very chic restaurants or the prices of rental apartments – nestles around the tranquil dual bay east of Darling Point. The patrons of the smartest sidewalk cafe tether their poodles to the wrought-iron tables while animatedly discussing who's wearing what, where and with whom. Here bottle-blondes with bronzed skin trying their best to look a couple of decades younger, European-looking emigrés with a penchant for Austrian pastries and the cosmopolitan life, and cool young things who drive Saabs enliven the scene.

New South Head Road climbs up from Double Bay, a gruelling part of the annual City to Surf Run when tens of thousands of Sydneysiders run, jog or walk the 14-kilometre (8.7-mile) stretch from the city to the famous surfing beach at Bondi. Then it drops down to Rose Bay, which is home to the Royal Motor Yacht Club, and climbs again to Vaucluse, where Vaucluse House nestles in 11 hectares (27 acres) of harbourside lawns and gardens. From 1829 to 1853, this battlemented Gothic residence was the home of William Charles Wentworth, father of the Australian Constitution and a member of the first expedition successfully to breach the Blue Mountains. The tearoom has a reputation for fine Devonshire teas.

The best-known eating establishment in the Eastern Suburbs, and probably Australia's most internationally recognised, is Doyles at the Fishermans Wharf at Watsons Bay, the last settlement on the southern harbour foreshores. Dining on seafood beside the little beach lined with upturned dinghies, looking out on the harbour which Mark Twain described as 'the darling of Sydney and the wonder of the world' is one of Sydney's essential travel experiences, and a fitting finale to a tour of the Eastern Suburbs.

ARCHITECTURE: FROM VICTORIAN TO ART DECO

'The most beautiful shopping centre in the world', a phrase coined by Pierre Cardin and promptly adopted as the Queen Victoria Building's catchphrase, may seem pretentious, but there is no denying that if it is not *the* best, QVB is certainly in the running. Natural light filters in through a majestic dome, an enormous barrel vault skylight and stained-glass windows to light up an entire city block of tiered shopping arcades. Bounded by George, Market, York and Druitt streets, the QVB was built in 1898 and owes its opulent, decorative character to the architect George McRae, who chose the Byzantine style in order to employ the many tilers, glaziers, stonemasons, and other craftsmen who were out of work because of a recession. In its original form, the QVB housed the city's main markets, shops, showrooms, a concert hall and a coffee palace, but later, when the overembellished Victorian style was considered passé, there were ill-conceived modernisations and threats of demolition. For decades it was boarded up, unused and unwanted, until it was revamped in the mid-1980s. Today, after a multimillion-dollar facelift which has maintained the QVB's original integrity, it is one of Sydney's favourite destinations.

Even if shoppers can't afford the designer labels at the plush boutiques, they can marvel at the Royal Clock which hangs from the roof. This 1-tonne

The 55-metre-high (180-foot) clock tower of the Sydney Town Hall was built in 1869 during the reign of Queen Victoria.

timepiece, a replica of one at Balmoral Castle in Scotland, is embellished with scenes of the English monarchy and announces the hours with a quartet of trumpet-blowing heralds. Other memorabilia from the Victorian era include the replica crown jewels of Queen Victoria, famous paintings of her royal personage, and outside, facing the Town Hall, a bronze statue of the Empress of the Empire herself which once resided at the Irish Parliament in Dublin before being ousted by the Republicans.

A 'Victorian grotesquerie' with 'rabbit-warren facilities' was the description given to the Town Hall by a 1960s historian caught up in the modernist mood of that decade, when more historic buildings were razed than in any other era. Likened to a 'wedding cake in stone', no doubt because of its eclectic architecture – the work of 11 different designers – the Town Hall with its five tiers of columns, arches, domes and porticoes topped by a clock tower does bear a surprising resemblance to the epicurean centrepiece of a marital reception. In winter, when the horse chestnut trees on Druitt Street are skeletal and leafless, the city's coat of arms can be spied on the northern wall. Carved into the beige sandstone is the date 1886, with a sailing ship and a rising sun flanked by a sailor in Georgian breeches and an Aborigine, and the strange motto 'Take But Surrender', leading one to muse on its historical consequences: Who did the taking and who the surrendering?

St Andrew's Cathedral, adjacent to the Town Hall, completes the Victorian trilogy at this end of the city. The original foundation stone for this Gothic Revival house of worship, said to have been influenced by England's York Minster, was laid by Governor Macquarie in 1819, but it was not until almost five decades later that the cathedral was finally consecrated.

Another architectural remnant from the high Victorian era survives nearby in somewhat surprising surroundings. The Marble Bar, the *pièce de résistance* of George Adams' Tattersall's Hotel, was rescued when the hotel was demolished in the 1960s. Everything, including the bronzes, marbles, fireplaces, and even the colonnaded entrance, was carefully numbered and reinstalled in the Sydney Hilton Hotel. The juxtaposition of the two different styles couldn't be more acute. The Hilton, like most of its sister establishments the world over, embodies 1970s American brutalism, or as a fellow journalist once described it, 'CIA-style'. On the other hand, the Marble Bar is a Victorian whimsy of Italian Baroque, boasting hunting scenes, curvaceous women and bountiful flora.

On the fringes of Hyde Park, three blocks east of the Town Hall, is another outstanding example of Victoriana. The Great Synagogue on Elizabeth Street, built in 1878, is evidence that, contrary to popular opinion, Australia was a multicultural nation from its beginning. This twin-towered melange of Gothic and Byzantine styles boasts stained-glass windows, wrought-iron gates, panelled ceilings, and cast-iron internal columns.

Hyde Park's Avenue of Remembrance is shaded by enormous Moreton Bay fig trees, with maze-like buttresses and canopies that engulf the sky. At lunch-time, office workers strip down to shorts and jog along the avenue which is bordered at one end by the monolithic Art Deco Anzac Memorial and at the other

by a bronze Apollo atop the Archibald Fountain, which was named after its donor, Jules Archibald, a philanthropic publisher and journalist. The spacious lawns are a good place for city workers to share a sandwich, meet a lover, soak up fresh air or work on a suntan. Hyde Park is for everyone, including destitute hobos sharing a bottle and their homespun philosophies on a park bench.

Overlooking the north-east corner of Hyde Park, and totally dominating the surroundings, is the Gothic-style St Mary's Cathedral. The author Jan Morris speculates that it was probably the British Empire's

Sydney's longest arcade, The Strand, was restored to its original Victorian splendour in 1980 after it was gutted by fire

largest church ever built outside the motherland. It is certainly enormous, which explains the length of time it took to build. Construction started in 1866 and although it was opened in 1882, work was still going on until 1928. The original plans by the architect, William Wardell, featured a couple of lofty western spires, and some presumptuous Victorian etchings even show them on city views. Due to lack of funds they were never built until a fund-raising campaign in the late 1990s finally made Wardell's vision a reality.

Just down the road, on the corner of College and William streets, is the Australian Museum. Built expressly as a museum, this sandstone building houses one of the world's best collections of natural history. When it opened in 1849, the director lived on the premises in a specially designed wing.

Facing Elizabeth Street, on the western side of Hyde Park, is Sydney's most famous department store, David Jones, or 'DJs' as it is commonly dubbed. There are other well-known chain stores, but none have the style of

DJs, renowned for its service, its lavish Christmas decorations, its lift operator announcing the different floors, and its original 1920s edifice which includes Italian marble floors. It is Sydney's answer to Harrods, and one of the last survivors of the grand age of department stores which began at the end of the 19th century and continued until the late 1950s. Some stores, like Grace Bros. on Broadway, covered an entire city block and were well-known landmarks built in enduring styles which contrast sadly with the plastic-looking malls of today. Prior to the 1960s, everyone went to the city to shop. Free musical performances and art exhibitions provided the entertainment, which culminated at Christmas when the stores vied with each other to stage the best pantomime.

The city's best shops are still located around DJs in the grid bordered by George, Elizabeth, Market and King streets, and while many are housed in characterless plate-glass boxes, the Strand Arcade, connecting George and Pitt streets, still preserves its elegant Victorian character. Destroyed by fire in

1976, the arcade has been restored to its original glory and now houses 80 boutiques, complete with stained-glass windows and wrought-iron balustrades.

Gilt ceilings, marble columns, bronze statues, enormous chandeliers and a magnificent mosaic floor combine to create a fantastically baroque effect at the State Theatre in Market Street. Built with a million-dollar price tag in the movie-mad 1920s, the theatre was advertised as the greatest in the British Empire, a boast which seems entirely believable even today, especially while viewing a stage show, when the interior of the theatre often seems just as spectacular as the events on stage.

Like a couple of giant golden cotton reels atop a spear, the undeniable and inescapable Sydney Tower thrusts from Centrepoint Arcade on Pitt Street and soars 300 metres (984 feet) above the city. The tower's controversial architectural merit is usually overlooked by visitors who are generally enthralled by the spectacular aerial views it affords of the city and far beyond.

Heading down George and Pitt streets towards Circular Quay, the broad sweep of Martin Place – the hub of the central business district – is now a pedestrian mall flanked by sleek, polished walls of granite housing the nation's premier banking institutions. At the George Street end, the Colonial Mutual Life Building with its arched facade is reminiscent of the city's turn-of-the-century commercial architecture, while on the corner of Elizabeth Street the contemporary, 1980s-style State Bank Centre, with its gleaming pink granite walls, 10-storeyed atrium and 36-storeyed office tower, provides a striking contrast. At the sunken auditorium in the middle of Martin Place, lunchtime concerts offer a welcome respite for stressed office workers. Looking down on this from her pedestal on the General Post Office, is a benign Queen Victoria flanked by a helmeted warrior and a bare-breasted maiden, in that bizarre style favoured by 19th-century artisans. Crowned by a fine clock and bell tower with an arcaded ground floor, the GPO is generally considered to be the best work of the colonial architect James Barnet. This superb example of Venetian Renaissance style is a fitting site to complete a tour of the city's architectural landmarks.

BEGUILING BEACHES

Sydneysiders have a passion for the beach. This preoccupation, which grips people from all walks of life and remains with them all their lives, often astounds outsiders by its intensity, but it is more easily understood when one considers that along the Pacific Ocean coastline of the city's suburbs are no fewer than 34 world-class beaches.

Bondi, with its expanse of sands and close proximity to the city, is the most internationally renowned of Sydney's beaches, but it is better known to Sydneysiders for its lively cafe scene, and is *the* place for young professionals to set up house. Manly, connected to the city by a harbour ferry service, is also easily accessible and extremely popular, but there are dozens more beaches to choose from, ranging from ritzy Palm Beach at the far end of the northern beaches to Cronulla, the family favourite, in the south.

On any summer weekend, in houses all over Sydney, the same ritual is enacted. The kids put on their 'cossies' (Aussie vernacular for a swimming costume) and the car is loaded with the canvas beach umbrella, mountains of towels, hats, and the trusty 'Esky' – a foam-lined food cooler filled with sandwiches and drinks. The surfboards are tied onto the roof, and the family heads off to the beach. On a blazing hot day when the red-roofed Western Suburbs can easily register 40° C (over 100° on the old Fahrenheit scale), the journey to the coast resembles an

Located only 8 kilometres (5 miles) from the city centre, Bondi, Sydney's best-known beach, is famed for its spacious sands and excellent surfing, and attracts thousands of beach-lovers on hot summer days.

The Baths at the southern end of Bondi Beach is the home of the Bondi Iceberg Club. Members are famed for braving this unheated ocean pool even on the coldest days of winter.

exodus, and on many a hot weekend Sydney's entire population appears to have relocated to the coastal strip.

Many a Sydneysider was first taught to swim in the saltwater pools, many of which still survive, on the headlands of the city's beaches. After learning the rudiments there, often as big seas swept over the baths, they graduated to the surf where the older generations passed on their skills in the fine art of body-surfing. This particular sport owed its origins to a Polynesian gardener named Tommy Tanna, who worked in Manly in the 1890s and astonished the locals by swimming out to sea, where he caught waves and rode them in to the shore. Fred Williams, one of the entranced teenagers who came to watch Tanna, became the first white man to take up bodysurfing and he was the doyen of the 'shooters' for half a century. Thousands took it up in later decades.

Given that there is such a variety of beaches, Sydneysiders have a wonderful choice, but most beachgoers have their favourites to which they return again and again, like a familiar restaurant. This theory discounts surfboard riders, however, as they are constantly on the prowl for good surf, and wind and wave conditions determine which beach they

will head for. The beaches are basically divided into two divisions, northern and southern, demarcated by the harbour. The southside beaches begin at Bondi, Australia's most famous stretch of sand and sea, so it is only fitting that our tour also starts from here.

Southside Beaches

Bondi, being closest to the city, has always drawn the biggest crowd, especially in the mid-century years when the tram ran directly to the beach. In the 1930s, when most Sydneysiders didn't own a car, 40 000 beachgoers on a summer weekend was not uncommon, with sunbathers shoulder to shoulder. In the early days, when swimmers wore voluminous bathing suits and were unaccustomed to the rips and undertows which are part and parcel of swimming in the surf, there were many drownings. In response, surf-lifesaving clubs were formed by the strongest swimmers, including Manly's Cecil Healy, who at that time held the world record for the 100-yards freestyle. The British-style 'surf pole', from which ropes went out to the drowning victim, was not suitable for Sydney's much larger beaches, so the surf-reel — a large version of a cotton

reel with rope wound around it — was invented at Bondi. A lifesaver, known as the beltman, wearing a cork-filled vest, would swim out with the rope to the person in distress and they would then be reeled in by a team of life-savers on the beach. Not surprisingly, these macho men with their bronzed, hulk-like bodies were the idols of their time. A cartoon in a British newspaper of 1935 shows dozens of fashionable women lined up under a billboard advertising that 'Rescue Patients are wanted for Australian Life-Savers'. But underneath the glamour, their purpose was deadly serious. Alwyn Moore, a former Bondi lifesaver, recalls being on duty on Black Sunday, the most notorious event in the history of Sydney's beaches. On 6 February 1938, a typical summer Sunday at Bondi, when the crowds were estimated at 35 000, several large waves rolled in in quick succession, sweeping hundreds of bathers off a sandbank and into a deep channel. There was mass hysteria as thousands of onlookers made the situation worse by trying to help in the rescues. Alwyn was one of the human chain of life-savers who worked to keep the large crowds at bay while the beltmen swam furiously through the mob to rescue those in the worst difficulty. Hundreds were hauled in, and although five people drowned (the first surf fatalities in Bondi's life-saving history), the rescue is still regarded as the greatest mass rescue in the history of world lifesaving.

Heading south from Bondi is tiny Tamarama where topless is *de rigueur* and body-watching is more popular than bodysurfing. Next is Bronte with its tree-lined park, a favourite venue for family picnics, then Clovelly, a rock beach popular with divers, down to Coogee where actor Mel Gibson used to play, and on to Maroubra for good surfing breakers. South of here is Long Bay, better known for its gaol than its sands, and adjacent Little Bay, which the internationally renowned sculptor Christo, in his trademark style, once completely wrapped as a 'living-sculpture'. Botany Bay sweeps the coastline away from the ocean and boasts some quiet swimming – waveless but not soundless, as the peace is constantly shattered by jets taking off from the international runway which juts out into the bay. Past Botany Bay is Cronulla, Sydney's longest beach, which at its northern end boasts some desert-like dunes that served as a substitute for Arabia in an early Australian movie.

Northside Beaches

North of the harbour the surf beaches begin at Manly, which is almost as well known as Bondi. The soaring Norfolk Island pines, Manly's signature for over a century, are suffering from pollution, but the beach, with its esplanade and the nearby Corso fringed with sidewalk cafes and fun parlours, is still one of Sydney's great escapes. Even on a winter Sunday, nutbrown bodies with pulp novels in hand worship the sun, a volleyball game goes on nearby, and teenagers rollerblade along the esplanade. Offshore, a lifesaver in a rubber duckie thumps over the swells, and an energetic octogenarian braves the chilly waters for his daily plunge. It is hard to imagine that just before he was born, in the early days of this century, swimming on Sydney's beaches in daylight hours was forbidden by law. During the repressive Victorian and Edwardian eras when exposing the body was considered indecent, bathing machines – wooden cubicles pulled by horses – would take the bather into the deeper water where he or she could discreetly immerse themselves. The Aussie version differed from the British model in that it was fitted with a wire enclosure to protect the bather from marauding sharks, a menace that was unknown in the colder European waters.

Turn-of-the-century photos show that Sydney's beaches were already a favourite venue with the growing populace. Thousands flocked there to take in the healthy air, and children paddled in the shallows. By 1903, William Gocher, the editor of a Manly newspaper, had had enough of the outmoded laws. He announced in his paper that he was going to defy the

Dressed in their characteristic Bondi colours, this group of volunteer lifesavers participates in surf rescues and carries on the tradition which began in the early 1900s.

ban publicly and swim in daylight hours. Gocher was arrested on his third successive Sunday bathe in the sea, but the magistrate decided against his conviction and the law was then rescinded, provided that the swimmers wore neck-to-knee costumes and the ladies took care not to expose even a hint of cleavage. Ironically, the Manly ratepayers who had backed the ban for so long found that only five years after Gocher's swim, property values had tripled and Manly's population had grown by 50 per cent. Everyone, it seemed, wanted to live near the beach, and it is very much the same today.

Freshwater, or Harbord as it is also known, located just north of Manly, is revered by surfers the world over as the beach where surfboard riding first made its Australian appearance when Duke Kahanamoku, the Hawaiian who won the gold medal for swimming at the 1912 Olympics, arrived in 1915. He was surprised that there were no board-riders on these beautiful hollow waves, so, undeterred by the fact that there were no surfboards in Australia, he purchased a length of pine and skilfully carved his own. After paddling out through the surf at Freshwater

Beach, he gave an exhibition of surfboard riding that so inspired Sydneysiders that they were immediately smitten. In the early days, though, the surfboards were heavy and ungainly, and were only manageable by muscled lifesavers. As a result, the sport was slow to develop until the Californian craze of malibu boards

A surfer attempts a cutback – going out of a wave and then coming back into it.

reached Sydney in the late 1950s, and then, with the baby boomers reaching their teens in the 1960s, surfing took off with a vengeance. 'The surfers', as the board-riding set dubbed themselves, literally became the new-wave idols of the beach, overtaking the lifesavers.

Parents despaired as their children answered the call of the surf, while lifesaving clubs were hard-pressed to get young people to join up. 'It'll never last,' said the doubters of the new sport. Thirty years later, surfing is, if anything, bigger than it ever was in the past. Australians still consistently win international titles, surf clothes are *the* fashion for beachgoers (even if they have never surfed), there are surfing millionaires, and the prize money at surf contests keeps going up.

Travelling north from Freshwater is Curl Curl, a long beach fringed by a grassy reserve, then Dee Why, which occasionally turns on a huge surf rolling off the point, up to Long Reef backed by a golf course. Collaroy, around the next point, is secluded and safe, while at the other end is North Narrabeen, renowned for its reliable surf in a north-easterly wind. Around the headland further north is protected Warriewood, and also Mona Vale which offers good surfing waves, a saltwater pool and The Basin, a quiet cove on its northern side. After Mona Vale, the prestigious residential area known as 'The Peninsula' begins. This 15-kilometre-long (9-mile) promontory is fringed by some of Sydney's most scenic beaches on its oceanic front, while the tranquil waterway of Pittwater laps up to its western foreshores. Yachts outnumber the houses in the leafy, well-heeled retreats of Pittwater, such as Church Point, Bayview and Clareville, and on tiny Scotland Island the residents live an idyllic existence. No cars are allowed on the island and the inhabitants use boats to get to the mainland, but they have the best of two worlds as the city centre is only a 40-minute bus ride away.

Bungan Beach, north of Mona Vale, is only accessible down a steep parkway,

This aerial photograph shows the traffic artery to the western suburbs, the elevated Western Distributor, snaking from the city across Darling Harbour to the suburb of Pyrmont.

which is its biggest attraction, while Newport, the next in line, attracts big weekend crowds because of its strip of restaurants and fish and chips shops. Pretty Bilgola nestles in a wooded cove with opulent beach houses lining its sands, while Avalon turns on a great surf, as does Whale Beach with its famous rocky outcrop known as 'The Wedge' which produces the waves that surfers love. Palm Beach, the last of the northern beaches, is the most exclusive, with its residents comprising a sizeable slab of Sydney's 'Who's Who'. Fringed by the cabbage tree palms which gave it its name, the quiet waters are protected on its southerly end, but are better for surfing in the north. Dominating Barrenjoey Head at Sydney's northernmost extremity is a lighthouse built in 1881 by the architect of the city's GPO, James Barnet. Walkers to the top of Barrenjoey are justly rewarded by one of Sydney's most fabulous vistas, encompassing the Ku-ring-gai Chase National Park overlooking Broken Bay and Pittwater to the west, with Lion Island and the bushland and beaches of the Central Coast to the north.

With such a wealth of beaches, most born-and-bred Sydneysiders admit that the sound of the surf is an essential ingredient to life in the city. These days, with the ever-present spectre of skin cancer, there is a drive to shun the sun. Government-sponsored programs try to educate beachgoers about the dangers of too much sun, but despite all this, the beach still beckons.

HEADING WEST TO PARRAMATTA

Sydney's western suburbs begin at the Town Hall, stretch westward 60 kilometres (37 miles) to the foothills of the Blue Mountains and number in their hundreds. Once thought of as a monotonous cultural desert of red-roofed brick veneers and industrial complexes, the west is now asserting itself and forging a new identity. In the inner west, old warehouses are being converted into spacious open-plan apartments. Further out, former industrial areas like Homebush Bay, the site of the 2000 Olympics, have been reinvented.

Darling Harbour

For almost a century and a half, Darling Harbour, named after the tyrannical 19th century governor Major General Ralph Darling, was a hive of maritime activity. Now the bay plays host to the city's premier tourist and convention centre, but the nautical flavour remains. On a clear winter Sunday, crowds of locals and tourists stroll around the promenade which flanks the glittering bay backed by the clean curved lines of Philip Cox's futuristic architecture. At the city end is the popular Sydney Aquarium, where visitors can walk underneath the harbour to view sharks and over 350 other fish species, while at the far end of the promenade is the National Maritime Museum, with nautical exhibits running the gamut from a history of beach fashions to a tour of the navy gunship *Vampire*. Sydney's first casino is located in Star City, the glittering harbourside complex adjacent to Darling Harbour. The futuristic monorail snakes across the harbour on the old Pyrmont Bridge, a steel structure built in 1902. At the waterfront cafes and glass-fronted food bars of Harbourside, an international clientele snacks on a menu which is just as multi-national. At the city's largest conglomeration of souvenir shops, shoppers can pick up a road sign warning 'Koalas Cross Here', record

their own video clip, or shop for opals. The Cockle Bay Wharf, opposite, is the latest edition to Darling Harbour and hosts stylish waterside restaurants and nightclubs. In the adjoining 50 hectares (123 acres) of once derelict land, Tumbalong Park is devoted to indigenous species, and next-door is the largest Chinese garden outside of mainland China, an appropriate introduction to nearby Chinatown.

Chinatown and surrounds

Dixon Street, the old hub, is full of restaurants and tourists, but the real action is now on adjoining Sussex and George streets, where Asian grocers stock once exotic greens that are now becoming household names, and where traditional apothecaries dispense roots, bones and leaves for herbal cures. Entire Asian-Australian families from all over Sydney converge here for the action, to dine on yum cha lunches, to stock up on Taiwanese videos, to buy cooking ingredients which are hard to find in the outer suburbs, but most of all to be part of the *reh-nau*, which translates as 'hot and noisy' – the bustle, noise and general bedlam of civilisation beloved by most Chinese.

At the foot of Chinatown is Paddy's Market, once known as the Haymarket, the city's major food market and

Dixon Street, the hub of Chinatown, is famed for its Chinese restaurants.

Chinatown's *raison d'être*. Later, Mediterranean migrants controlled the great vaulted market, but since the removal of the city's food markets further west to Flemington, Paddy's has become a huge weekend flea market. Other nearby attractions include the Pumphouse Brewery Tavern, a restored pumphouse and brewery with a popular outdoor tavern, the Sydney Entertainment Centre, and the Powerhouse Museum on Harris Street, Ultimo, which is by all accounts one of the world's most entertaining museums. The dramatic architecture of the museum, which celebrates technology, science and the arts, incorporates the old boiler house and the turbine hall, original brick structures over 80 metres (262 feet) long and 28 metres (92 feet) wide.

At Railway Square is Central Station, a rambling sandstone station with vaulted halls in the Victorian tradition, topped by a clock tower. Before the Harbour Bridge was built in the 1930s and the underground railway extended further into the city, Central lived up to its name as the city's hub, and huge department stores catered to the hordes of customers from the suburbs and the bush who alighted at the station. The turreted former Grace Bros building on Broadway, which still survives, is spread over an entire city block, and was

Completed for Sydney's Bicentenary in 1988, the Darling Harbour urban development program succeeded in transforming an obsolete dockland into a vibrant recreational complex.

among the area's businesses which suffered from a reversal of fortunes. But with the inner city renaissance many of the old warehouses have now been restored and revamped as highly sought after apartments.

Inner West

Parramatta Road, one of the city's busiest arteries and the traditional route to the west, begins at Victoria Park. The University of Sydney, Australia's oldest and most prestigious font of academia with its ivy-covered halls and an Oxbridge-style quadrangle, sprawls for a kilometre along the southern side of Parramatta Road, while to the north is Glebe. This turn-of-the-century suburb is renowned for its restaurants, bookshops, historic architecture and an eclectic population which embraces radicals, alternatives, students, those in creative fields, 'yuppies', and families who have lived in the area for generations. This 160-hectare (395-acre) parcel of land which was the original 'glebe' – property given by the church for the use of the clergy – was first designated in the colony's earliest days. In the 1820s the harbour frontages were sold off as large estates, but then in the 1840s these were subdivided and the middle classes moved in, while the poor lived in hovels in the swampy lowlands. This geographical

hierarchy is evident in Glebe's surviving architecture. Up on the heights is the three-storeyed St Scholastica's College, originally built in 1831 for the solicitor George Allen, son of King George III's physician, who founded Sydney's first law firm. Part of its former vast grounds are now part of the Harold Park Raceway. Visits of famous people to this old mansion include the visit in 1881 of the prince who later became King George V, and that of Pope Paul in 1970. The surrounding leafy streets are a medley of Victorian and Federation houses, well worth exploring, and at the end of your tour there is the culinary reward of browsing through the black-board menus of over 40 eateries along Glebe Point Road, one of Sydney's restaurant capitals.

Across Blackwattle Bay is the formerly industrial Pyrmont which is being remodelled into a residential and commercial development. The inner city's latest landmark, the Golden Gate-like Anzac Bridge spans Blackwattle Bay, once an industrial area of Pyrmont, which is now a revamped resedential and commercial area. On its shores is Sydney Fish Market, a favourite place to not only bury seafood but also to enjoy it by the wharves. Rambling over the peninsula to the north of the bridge is Balmain, a suburb which, like Paddington in the east,

has had a chequered history. Named after William Balmain, the doctor who was first given a 220-hectare (543-acre) land grant there in 1800, Balmain later became a fashionable suburb in the Victorian era because it was only a short ferry ride to the city. The homes of many of the city's illustrious sons and daughters still survive here, including Hampton Villa, the home of Henry Parkes – the 'Father of Federation' – and the Manor House, now a restaurant, the original residence of Edmund Blacket who designed the Great Hall of Sydney University and the Garrison Church at The Rocks. After a shipyard was built in the mid-19th century, Balmain became less fashionable and until its rediscovery in the 1960s, it was a typical working-class enclave famed for its unionists, pubs on every street corner and independent, resourceful inhabitants.

The best way to enjoy the journey through the western suburbs to Parramatta is to forego the usually overcrowded highway and board one of the RiverCats at Circular Quay for a scenic trip up the Parramatta River. On the southern shore, past Balmain, are Drummoyne and Abbotsford, linked by the 16-kilometre-long (10-mile) Foreshore Walkway completed for the Bicentennial in 1988. Attractions include delightful parks and bays, the Sydney Rowing Club – home of Australia's Olympic rowers – and the waterfront homestead where the nation's best-known poet, 'Banjo' Paterson, who penned 'Waltzing Matilda' and 'The Man From Snowy River', once lived.

Across the water on the northern shore is Hunters Hill, the city's original 'garden suburb' and one of its most elegant and best-preserved residential areas. Shaded by century-old camphor laurels are old sandstone mansions draped in wisteria and Georgian-style cottages with English-style gardens.

At Homebush Bay, further upriver, 800 hectares (1977 acres) of former industrial land has been transformed into Sydney's 2000 Olympics site, a magnificent sporting complex of stadiums, parklands and athletic centres including an International Aquatic

The Sydney International Aquatic Centre built for the 2000 Olympics at the Homebush Olympic site features underwater viewing and a leisure area with spas and a water slide.

Built in 1793 as the home of John and Elizabeth Macarthur, Elizabeth Farm at Parramatta is Australia's oldest building. Now a museum, it contains the paintings and canopied beds owned by the Macarthurs, who were pioneers in the Australian wool industry.

Centre, the giant Stadium Australia, residential complexes and a connecting railway. The new Sydney Showground, home to the famed Royal Agricultural Society's Royal Easter Show, is also part of the Homebush Bay site. The adjacent Bicentennial Park, a 90-hectare (222-acre) parkland of indigenous trees and shrubs. A 5-kilometre-long (3-mile) boardwalk winds through the park's extensive mangrove forests which cover approximately 50 hectares (123 acres) of wetlands.

Parramatta

At the 'head of the river', which some etymologists claim is the true translation of the city's Aboriginal name, lies Parramatta. The most popular meaning of the name Parramatta is 'the place where eels gather'. The reason for this popular acceptance could be that the Rugby League home team uses this teleost fish as its symbol. Parramatta is Australia's second-oldest settlement, having been founded only three months after the First Fleet landed in Sydney Cove. Because its river flats were more suitable for agriculture than the rocky shores of Sydney Harbour, crops flourished here. The colony's first wheat, barley and maize were harvested in 1789; Parramatta's other agriculturally

related debuts include the first orchard, vineyard, winery, tannery, and brewery. An enormous 12-kilogram (26-pound) cabbage was cut especially for the King's birthday celebrations. Buoyed up by its agricultural prowess, Parramatta's population actually exceeded that of Sydney for a short while at the end of the 18th century.

The original settlement was at Crescent Hill in what is now Parramatta Park behind Government House. This Georgian-style vice-regal residence originally served as a country retreat. First built in 1790, Australia's oldest public building was rebuilt into its present structure nine years later. While in residence here during the spring months, the colony's governor received official news from his Sydney office via flag signals. Government House was enlarged in 1815 by Macquarie as part of his extensive building program, which included laying out the central grid of Parramatta, building the Colonial Hospital, parts of which still survive at Parramatta Hospital, and building the Female Factory where the 'poor, the ugly, the mad, the old, the wizened' were sent, according to the historian Robert Hughes. It is now part of Rydalmere Hospital.

Dating from 1793, Elizabeth Farm on Alice Street is reputed to be the oldest European building in the country and, with its deep verandahs shaded by a wide roof, it is generally thought to be the forerunner of the typical Australian homestead. It was formerly the residence of John and Elizabeth Macarthur, who were responsible for pioneering the hugely successful merino wool industry in Australia. The heritage home and the tea-house are surrounded by a pretty 19th-century cottage garden.

The third-oldest settlement in Australia is Windsor, once a farming district on the Hawkesbury River. Now, like its neighbouring sister settlement of Richmond, it is being engulfed by the great westerly suburban sprawl. Governor Macquarie laid out both of these towns and a number of the historic buildings still survive, notably the Greenway-designed St Matthew's Anglican Church at Windsor with its great square tower and the most fascinating collection of early gravestones in the Sydney area. Some other heritage buildings in this town include Greenway's sandstone courthouse (1822) and the Tebbutt house and observatory (1845) which is still owned by the original family.

THE BLUE MOUNTAINS

To stand on the viewing platform at Echo Point in the Blue Mountains, about 100 kilometres (62 miles) west of Sydney, and gaze out upon the world-renowned panorama is perhaps the most memorable experience to be found within a day's drive of Sydney. The huge Jamison Valley fans out from the lookout, and enclosing it as far as the eye can see are vertical sandstone cliffs of flesh and apricot tones which appear particularly splendid at sunrise or sunset. To the left are the Three Sisters, triplet geological obelisks, siblings turned to stone in Aboriginal legend, and below are the vast rainforests of the 200 000-hectare (494 200-acre) Blue Mountains National Park. Most people assume that the Blue Mountains fulfil the normal ideal of mountains, but they are actually a series of sandstone plateaus dissected by gorges and forested river valleys.

Artefacts unearthed by archaeologists show that Aborigines have inhabited the Blue Mountains for at least 20 000 years; however, the first Europeans to sight them in June 1789, 18 months after the founding of Sydney, named the range after its distinctive colouring.

Botanists later discovered that this is caused by a blue haze created when light passes through the droplets of oil discharged from the eucalyptus trees.

A highway climbs effortlessly from the suburban plains of western Sydney up through the mountains, making it hard to imagine that this range was once considered impassable. The early settlers were eager to see what was beyond the mountains, but explorers were turned back by cliffs which blocked them at every turn. Their attempts are still remembered by their names. Dawes Ridge marks where William Dawes tried in vain to conquer the barrier in 1789. Francis Barrallier, namesake of Barrallier Falls, befriended the Gandangara Aborigines who wore cloaks of kangaroo skins, but their territory was to the south of the ridges and they didn't know the secret of how to cross the mountains. The Daruk people lived on the plateau, which was a separate territory, and it is rumoured that an escaped convict by the name of John Wilson crossed the mountains with them in 1798 – but with no proof, the tale remains a legend.

In 1811, Gregory Blaxland, a free settler in pursuit of grasslands for his sheep, went on a preliminary exploration. He returned convinced that if an expeditionary party stayed on the crowning ridge, the mountains could be crossed as all previous attempts through the valleys had been thwarted by the box canyons. He convinced William Charles Wentworth, a native-born civil servant, and William Lawson, a surveyor, that his plan would be successful. Imbued with a mixture of curiosity, a need for grasslands and a hankering after fame, the trio, together with four servants, several dogs, and pack horses laden with provisions, set out on 11 May 1813. The forests were so dense that paths had to be cut each day before the horses could proceed, and the explorers were stunned that the climate was so different from that of the eastern plains. In the morning thick frosts covered the ground, and a kangaroo leg kept for dog meat was frozen solid. Blaxland showed his gloomy spirits when he wrote in his journal that the mountains were like 'dreadful convulsions of nature', and when noises were heard at night he was convinced that natives were intending to spear them. They passed a pile of stones erected by an earlier explorer who had concluded that 'it was impossible to find a passage even for a person on foot', but doggedly they pressed on until the 20th day, when they stood on the last ridge and gazed west across boundless grassy plains. Wentworth later remarked that

Viewed from a scenic lookout at Katoomba, the Blue Mountains National Park stretches to the horizon and comprises a vast area of box canyons, eucalyptus forests, rainforested gullies, and spectacular waterfalls.

Rhododendrons thrive in the cool, moist climate of the Blue Mountains, especially at Blackheath where the colourful Rhododendron Gardens are a major attraction.

he had felt what he imagined the Israelites had felt when they first viewed Canaan, their Promised Land.

The successful explorers were given vast land grants for their efforts and their names are immortalised by the townships of Blaxland, Wentworth Falls and Lawson. A year later a road was built close to the original route, but it was not until the railway was completed in 1867 that the Blue Mountains were finally 'discovered'. Sydneysiders flocked up on the trains to marvel at the spectacular scenery, bushwalking became a popular pursuit – particularly because the mountain air was said to be a health tonic – and the wealthy built their retreats overlooking the best views.

In Katoomba, the capital of the mountains, Victorian and Edwardian boarding houses perch above the terraced streets, and around the spectacular Cliff Drive to Leura are gracious old homes with picket-fenced cottage gardens shaded by pines, maples and rhododendrons. During the spring and autumn when the gardens are at their best, many of these historical retreats are open to the public. At Leura is 'Everglades' where bluebells and daffodils bloom in spring, while at Wentworth Falls is 'Yester Grange', built in 1886 for a retired sea captain. It is renowned not only for its gardens and views but for its amazing collection of Victorian memorabilia. There are stuffed parrots, lyrebirds and albatrosses, original antique furniture, historical photographs including a 5.5-metre-long (18-foot) panorama of Queen Victoria's coronation procession, and a glasshouse tearoom which overlooks a garden of autumnal splendour and serves fresh warm scones with real whipped cream.

Bushwalking has always been one of the major attractions of the mountains and there are hundreds of trails ranging from half-kilometre strolls to arduous week-long treks. The National Pass walk built around the turn of the century is arguably one of the best trails. This 4-kilometre (2.5-mile) circuit follows a rock ledge halfway down the cliff face, with views of some of the region's most spectacular scenery. From the township of Wentworth Falls, sandstone steps climb down to the Empress Falls where ferns thrive and rosellas chatter in the sassafras trees. The track winds around the cliff ledge under and over waterfalls, past tea-trees and gnarled bonsai trees growing from rock crevices against all odds. From the lookouts the views are awesome, as is the 300-metre-high (984-foot) climb up from the valley floor beside the spectacular Wentworth Falls.

Most tourists who come to the Blue Mountains take a ride on the near-vertical Scenic Railway (originally built in 1885 to transport coal and miners) which claims to be the world's steepest railway; and they board the Skyway, an aerial cable car, for a heart-stopping ride 275 metres (900 feet) above the Jamison Valley. But to experience the full majesty of the region, nothing beats a bush walk down into those silent valleys where the eucalypt forests tower overhead and the waterfalls crash down from the sandstone cliffs. In such a setting it is easy to imagine that you are back in the days of the early explorers, for little has changed in the valleys since those early days. Not so, though, in the towns of the plateau which have been steadily increasing in size ever since the first settlers were lured here by the wonderful views and the cool, crisp climate. But, despite the proliferation of modern blights such as motels and shopping malls, many historic buildings survive. At Katoomba there is the unique Paragon Cafe with its authentic 1930s Art Deco interior, and the Carrington Hotel, once dubbed the 'Honeymoon Capital of Australia'. Perched on a clifftop at Medlow Bath is the ornate Hydro-Majestic Hotel with its wondrous views over the Megalong Valley and an architectural style which has been described as 'an Edwardian folly with a touch of Art Deco'. However, the most popular historical attraction is the Norman Lindsay Gallery and Museum at Springwood, which is housed in the former house and studio of one of Australia's most versatile and controversial artists. Famed for his paintings of nudes and satyrs, his popular children's books and his bohemian lifestyle, Lindsay resided at his Springwood home for 60 years until his death in 1969.

Other attractions in the mountain region include the Rhododendron Gardens at Blackheath, the historic villages of Hartley and Little Hartley, the spectacular Kanangra Walls and the Jenolan Caves, 164 kilometres (100 miles) from Sydney. The entrance drive winds through Australia's largest open cave, the Grand Arch, to the historic mock-Tudor Caves House built in 1898. Guided tours explore many of the 22 major caves in the Jenolan system, renowned for its limestone formations.

The cool, green Kangaroo Valley, renowned for its fertile river plains, was first settled by pioneering cattlemen and their families in the 1820s.

A TASTE OF OLDE ENGLAND

In the green rolling meadows, black-and-white Friesian cows graze contentedly, overlooking a pastoral scene which is reminiscent of Europe. Roadways are lined with pines and deciduous trees, watercourses are fringed with weeping willows, and there are hedgerows of creamy-flowering privet, and gracious stone homes, their gardens ablaze with azaleas and magnolias. But for glimpses of higher rocky ground clad in the unmistakable grey-green of the Australian bush, the old-world illusion that the Southern Highlands presents is almost authentic. This region, which centres on the upmarket towns of Bowral and Moss Vale about 126 kilometres (78 miles) south-west of Sydney, was from the outset envisaged as a cool retreat for the gentry who were hankering after their English homelands.

The Southern Highlands seems a misnomer when approaching the area from the Hume Highway, as the elevation is so gradual. But from the South Coast, climbing up the Macquarie Pass to Robertson or up the escarpment from Kangaroo Valley, the elevation of this area is much more apparent, as is the climatic change – especially in winter when the coast can be quite mild while the highlands are covered in snow.

Mittagong, the first town visitors reach when approaching from the Sydney side, has lost most of its previous picturesque qualities with suburbanisation, but it still boasts Kennerton Green, which many horticulturists believe is Australia's finest private garden. Featuring sweeping lawns and woodlands massed with bluebells and freesias in spring, Kennerton Green also boasts superb Victorian-style geometric gardens. Nearby Bowral competes with its yearly tulip festival and a swathe of private gardens which are open to the public in spring and autumn, including the English-style parklands of Greenbrier Park, the avenues of flowering cherries at Riverside Park and the autumnal glory of the deciduous trees at Busker's End.

Bowral, often referred to as the 'Double Bay of the Southern Highlands', boasts a plethora of private schools, an electoral roll liberally sprinkled with names from Sydney's 'Who's Who', and a disproportionate number of upmarket coffee shops, restaurants, boutiques, and antique stores. On weekends, Bowral's main street is full of weekend farmers, from leading politicians to rock superstars, nicknamed the 'moleskin millionaires', as they stroll around town in their obligatory Akubra hats and oilskins while their cattle dogs ride in splendour in the backs of Jaguars and Mercedes. Since the 1920s it has become fashionable to retreat to the highlands and while away the summer playing golf and tennis. Milton Park, once the stately home of a department store dynasty, is now a prestigious hotel, while 'Craigieburn' hasn't changed its genteel veneer since fashionable families holidayed there in the 1930s. Bowral's most famous personality, however, is no social scion but the cricketer Donald Bradman, who hit the first of his renowned centuries at the Centennial Oval. He is immortalised at the Bradman Museum and by the playing fields that bear his name.

Berrima, south-west of Bowral, owes its mid-19th-century character to the fact that the railway bypassed it in 1860 and it subsequently declined until it was rediscovered a century later. The National Trust has listed the entire town as a national treasure, which is not surprising, considering that at least two dozen of Berrima's buildings are of historical significance. The notorious Berrima Gaol, the nation's oldest penal establishment still in operation, was built by convict labour in 1839, as was the Court House which dates from the same era and the Surveyor General Inn which has been continuously licensed since the 1830s. Many of the other old inns now function as restaurants and souvenir and craft shops, while Harper's Mansion has been restored to illustrate family life in Berrima during its Georgian heyday.

Moss Vale owes its existence to the Throsby family who first explored the area and were given a land grant in 1819. Throsby Park, a 27-roomed mansion dating from 1834 and the family seat for five generations, still survives on the outskirts of town. According to legend, Moss Vale was named after Jemmy Moss, a shepherd of the Throsby family who was the first European resident of the area. South of Throsby Park on the Illawarra Highway is the Tudor House school, where Nobel Prize-winning novelist, Patrick White, acquired his early schooling. The nearby hamlet of Sutton Forest centres on the elegant Royal Inn and a gallery-cum-antique store housed in the original butcher's shop. The road winds through pleasant rolling downs to Bundanoon, a congenial resort town bordering the Morton National Park on the edge of the escarpment. Bundanoon's heyday was in the 1930s and 1940s, before most Sydneysiders owned their own cars, and the town's guesthouses and hotels were filled to capacity every weekend when the city trains arrived. Bushwalking and the fresh mountain air were the major attractions, and even today these are still Bundanoon's drawcards. The nearby attractions are aptly described by names like Glow Worm Glen, Fairy Bower Falls, Fern Tree Gully, Grand Canyon, and Sunrise Point. Bundanoon's major annual event is Brigadoon, held every April. This Scottish celebration, complete with Highland games and pipe bands, would apparently suggest a Celtic connection with the town's name, but 'Bundanoon' comes from the Aboriginal word for 'deep gorges', which is a fitting description of the surrounding landscape.

East of Moss Vale, travellers can take the Illawarra Highway to Robertson, famed for its potatoes which thrive in the sepia-hued soil. This small town has the obligatory antique shops, coffee shops and an English-manor-style retreat, Ranelagh House, which was built in 1924. South-west of Robertson is Burrawang, a small historic village with an English ambience, a Gothic-style parsonage and a general store which has been trading for 130 years.

Tumbling 81 metres (265 feet) from the escarpment into the wilderness forests of the Morton National Park, Fitzroy Falls is one of the major scenic attractions of the Southern Highlands and boasts some wonderful picnic spots, a variety of bushwalking trails and spectacular lookouts.

Travellers can leave the highlands from here by continuing down a winding mountain pass to picturesque Kangaroo Valley and onwards to Berry on the South Coast. Alternatively they can exit from Robertson down the Macquarie Pass to Albion Park near Wollongong.

THE SOUTH COAST

Artists and writers have always been drawn to the South Coast, because of its spectacular scenery and because the region has a certain timeless ambience, a lifestyle which is less hurried and commercial than that of the North Coast. The English novelist D. H. Lawrence spent three months during the winter of 1922 writing *Kangaroo* at 'Wyewurk', a seaside bungalow at Thirroul which still stands at 3 Craig Street, while Australia's best-known contemporary artist, Brett Whiteley, kept returning to Thirroul for inspiration until his untimely death there in 1993. Arthur Boyd, another renowned artist, spends most of his time at 'Bundanon', 21 kilometres (13 miles) west of Nowra overlooking the Shoalhaven River. This historic homestead, with its studio featuring paintings embracing four generations of Boyds, has been bequeathed to the state government and is open to the public on certain days of the year, even though the family still resides there.

Travellers heading south from Sydney on the Princes Highway can take the Coast Road to Stanwell Park or the highway via Bulli Lookout. It is highly recommended to take the alternative route on the return journey as the panoramas are remarkable on both drives.

South of Sutherland a winding drive meanders through the Royal National Park, a route which is at its best during the winter and early spring wildflower season. The park offers extensive bushwalking trails, delightful picnic grounds and splendid beaches, and at the southern end where the road emerges from the bush at Stanwell Tops, the coastal panorama must rate among Australia's most superb vistas. High above Bald Hill, hovering in the updraughts created by this unique geographical phenomenon, are hang-gliders looking like giant rainbow-coloured birds. Members of the hang-gliding fraternity are not the first aviators to be drawn to the area, however, as the sleepy hamlet of Stanwell Park was once the home of Lawrence Hargrave, who invented the box kite and was at the forefront of Australia's aviation industry.

The road south winds down the mountain through groves of palms and pockets of rainforest, and then the coastal plain narrows until it disappears entirely where the mountains meet the sea. Carved into the cliff-face, the coastal road hangs above platforms of rock. Signs cautioning 'Do Not Stop' warn motorists of falling rocks and add an element of danger and a touch of Monty Pythonish humour to the route. A railway line pops out of the mountain and follows the road to the south, passing old mining villages like Coalcliff and Coaldale, where former miners' cottages are now sought-after seaside homes. Some of the collieries

Kiama is famed for its Blowhole. The source of its Aboriginal name means 'where the sea makes a noise'.

The site for the Nan Tien Temple at Berkeley was chosen by Buddhist priests because of its geomantic harmony.

are still operational, and are still as Lawrence described them: 'where the men just walked into the face of the hill down a tunnel, and they hardly disfigured the land at all.'

Off the point at Bulli, a group of surfboard riders bob in the surf like a flock of seagulls, while further out to sea a fleet of freighters waits to load up with coal, iron and steel, the lifeblood of the region. This combination of panoramic coastal vistas and industrial complexes may seem incongruous, but it provides some fascinating contrasts which are best appreciated when viewed from the top of the escarpment at Bulli Pass or while having a Devonshire tea at the tea-house perched on the top of the aptly named Sublime Point nearby.

Wollongong's foreshore drive loops past beaches, parklands and the original harbour, home port for a fleet of fishing trawlers, yachts and cruisers, and the location for seafood restaurants conveniently situated next to the fish market. 'The Steel City' also boasts its own university, an acclaimed botanical garden, as well as the largest Buddhist temple in the Southern Hemisphere. Built at a high cost, painted bright orange with red-tiled Chinese roofs and a matching pagoda, the Nan Tien Temple sprawls over 22 hectares (54 acres) of former industrial land at Berkeley, just south of Wollongong. The dual contrasts of this stretch of coastline are nowhere more apparent than at neighbouring Port Kembla, where the smokestacks of the steelworks overlook white beaches on one side and the Buddhist temple on the other.

Further south is Shellharbour, a popular surfing and fishing spot, and in the Jamberoo Valley, about 100 kilometres (62 miles) from Sydney, is the Minnamurra Falls National Park. Here visitors can appreciate the original rainforests that once thrived in the region before the timbercutters went to work in the early days, practically decimating species like cedar, which are only now making a comeback. The timber was shipped out from the harbour at nearby Kiama, a picturesque coastal town renowned for its blowhole, a natural rock formation that is at its most dramatic when a big sea is running and sprays can rise to over 50 metres (164 feet) into the air. In Aboriginal dialect, Kiama means 'the spot where the sea booms'.

Shamrock-green hills roll down to the ocean south of Kiama, and in the valleys around Gerringong, Berry and along the Shoalhaven River are some of the best dairy pastures in Australia. The suburban sprawl is starting to take over on the outskirts of Kiama, but there are still remnants of rock walls built by convicts over a century ago. Coral trees with their scarlet flowers and homesteads with traditional red roofs are familiar sights along the road to the historic town of Berry, named after the martinet pioneer Alexander Berry who died in 1873 aged 92. Berry's main street is lined with historic buildings now revamped into restaurants, shops and galleries. From Berry, travellers can journey south to Nowra and the beautiful shores of Jervis Bay further afield. An alternative route back north heads out to the coast via the historic winery at Coolangatta, and to the superb sands of Seven Mile Beach and adjacent Geroa, where Sir Charles Kingsford Smith took off on the first commercial flight across the Tasman to New Zealand. A third possibility is to follow the road over Cambewarra Mountain to Kangaroo Valley, a rural retreat for many of Sydney's rich and famous, and then continue up to Fitzroy Falls and return to Sydney via the Southern Highlands.

CENTRAL COAST AND HUNTER VALLEY

North of Newcastle, the state's second-largest city, the landscape alternates between extensive waterways and long lazy beaches – two of the main reasons why the Central Coast has always been such a popular escape from the city.

Hemming in the northern reaches of Sydney are the flooded valleys of the Hawkesbury River system which are now contained within the Ku-ring-gai Chase National Park. The river was first explored by Governor Arthur Phillip in the colony's earliest days, but it wasn't until the northern railway was built in 1889 and the Central Coast was finally linked to the city, that its transformation into a resort area came about. Even then progress was slow, and for decades the region was a collection of sleepy fishing villages and quiet seaside towns where city families built cheap cottages known as 'weekenders'. But in the 1960s the Central Coast's boom time began, a process which is still going on today.

From Hornsby in Sydney's north-west, travellers can opt for either the expressway, which burrows through sandstone hills and straddles the mountaintops offering spectacular panoramas of the Hawkesbury River, or they can take the meandering old Pacific Highway, which allows a quieter pace and a chance to stop off at Brooklyn, a popular stopover for river cruises, named after the nearby bridge over the Hawkesbury which resembles its New York namesake.

Gosford, the commercial heart of the Central Coast, is the jumping-off spot for the surrounding attractions, including scenic Avoca Beach, Bouddi National Park with its majestic cliffs and ocean views, Pearl Beach with its upmarket cafes and wealthy hideaways, and the Brisbane Water National Park outside Woy Woy, site of the well-preserved Bulgandry Aboriginal engravings.

The coastal strip from Terrigal to The Entrance has been a popular holiday destination for generations, but these days many of the old 'weekenders' are permanent residences, although the guesthouses and motels still cater for holiday-makers. Nowadays there are also more shopping malls and fast-food joints, but the beaches and lakes are still less crowded than those of Sydney. Despite the inevitable creep of suburbia, The Entrance still has a holiday feel to it, similar to an English beach resort. There are fun parlours, water slides, fish and chips shops, old guesthouses, shops crammed with shell art, and organised activities like pelican feeding. It's not trendy, but it's a lot of fun. The Entrance straddles a spit of land between the ocean and Tuggerah Lakes, and, as its name suggests, the town is situated where the lake spills into the Pacific. This waterway and the neighbouring Lake Budgewoi, Lake Munmorah and the expansive Lake Macquarie further north are popular for fishing, yachting, windsurfing or just lazing around on boats.

Newcastle is rarely explored by Sydneysiders, who usually drive past en route to the popular wineries of the Hunter Valley. Like Wollongong, its sister coal-and-steel city to the south, Newcastle suffers from an image problem, but for the traveller who ventures here there is a wealth of attractions.

Coal was first discovered on the banks of the Hunter River by runaway convicts almost a decade before Newcastle was established in 1804 as Australia's second mainland penal settlement. Irish dissidents were sent there to mine coal and cut the cedar which grew in vast stands throughout the Hunter Valley. This aromatic wood with its wonderful reddish-gold hue was used extensively for interiors in Governor Macquarie's building boom, and as a result the trees were logged out of existence by the 1820s. Luckily for Newcastle's future, the coal was more difficult to access and it is still the region's main *raison d'être*.

The commercial heart of the city is situated on a hilly promontory overlooking the Hunter River and backed by the Pacific Ocean, and the river foreshores have been landscaped into attractive parklands. Some of the prominent buildings on the city's skyline include the elegant City Hall built in 1929, with its cupola-topped clock tower, and the old Customs House tower, but the most dominant structure is the great Gothic-style Newcastle Cathedral on top of the hill. Construction

began in 1869 and has continued on and off until today (the cathedral's ambitious spire is still incomplete).

Along the riverside is a life-size replica of the first coastal steamer built in Australia, and from Queen's Wharf a ferry plies across the river to the industrial suburb of Stockton. The rocky promontory at the southern end of the harbour entrance, known as Nobbys Head, was once an island, while nearby Fort Scratchley was built in the 1870s to protect Newcastle from the improbability of a Russian invasion. It is now the Maritime and Military Museum, and is the only Australian mainland fort ever to have fired its guns in defence against an enemy when a Japanese submarine entered the harbour in 1942.

Newcastle is famous for its surfing beaches, which have produced many internationally renowned surfing champions, while the Ocean Baths with their wonderful Art Deco pavilion are reputed to be the largest in the Southern Hemisphere. Other attractions include the Victorian terrace houses, cafes and galleries of Cox Hill (the 'Paddington of Newcastle'), the nearby Newcastle Regional Art Gallery in an avenue of enormous fig trees and, on the shores of Lake Macquarie, the former house of one of Australia's best-known artists, William Dobell, which has been turned into a museum and a gallery of his work.

The Hunter Valley produces some of Australia's best-known wines, and a wine-tasting tour is an essential experience for a daytrip from Sydney. The old mining town of Cessnock, 50 kilometres (31 miles) west of Newcastle, is the gateway to this fertile region where grapes have been grown commercially since 1858. There are over 40 wineries scattered around the valley, which welcome visitors for wine-tasting; some of Australia's best-known labels are produced here. Many of the vineyards, like Hungerford Hill, offer restaurants, playgrounds for the kids and other diversions. But the Hunter Valley is really about wine-tasting, and for visitors who want to imbibe but not lose their driving licence there are special tours which offer daytrips or weekend jaunts.

Seven million grape vines swathe the rolling hills of the Hunter Valley and the region's famed wines are exported all over the world.

THE CITY AND THE HARBOUR

Opposite: *The Opera House, the crowning glory of Sydney Cove.*
Above: *Reflections of a modern city.*

There are few vistas in the world which can compete with the city of Sydney nestled around its breathtaking harbour. At the site of the city's humble foundation, just over two centuries ago, high-rise office towers cluster behind Sydney Cove. Despite their size, they are overshadowed by two magnificent modern icons: the Opera House with a gleaming white roof reminiscent of the yachts that crisscross the waters at its feet; and the powerful steel arch of the Harbour Bridge that links the north and south shores of this most picturesque waterway.

The deep ultramarine harbour, comprising over 55 square kilometres (21 square miles), meanders from the mouth of the Parramatta River, past Circular Quay where tubby green and yellow ferries radiate to all corners of the harbour, skirts the Botanic Gardens, past coves and bays filled with yachts and cruisers, and around small islands that dot the waterways, past the luxurious villas, bungalows and banks of apartments which teeter to the water's edge, and continues alongside the heathlands and cliffs that are part of the Sydney Harbour National Park to a mighty gateway, the North and South heads. These two sheer headlands curve in and act as sentinels beyond which lies the Pacific Ocean. It is little wonder that acerbic writer Clive James declared on his return to Sydney after 30 years abroad: 'Why didn't I spend my life down here?'

Australia's best-known, biggest, oldest and most beautiful and exciting city is home to an eclectic population of just over 3.7 million embracing nationalities from over 60 countries. Sydneysiders of Anglo-Celtic origin still make up the majority, but about a quarter of the city's inhabitants come from non-English-speaking backgrounds and Chinese is Sydney's second most spoken language with Arabic running a close third. The result of this multicultural influence makes Sydney the most cosmopolitan city of the Asia Pacific, boasting not only a flourishing arts and cultural scene, but a plethora of restaurants and cafes offering all the world's best cuisine. These culinary delights, combined with the city's feast of visual splendours, makes Sydney one of the world's most popular tourist destinations.

Previous pages: Circular Quay is the hub of the city. Ferries crisscross the harbour, connecting the Quay to the suburbs, and these routes pass some of the grandest homes and the most beautiful secluded inlets and bays.

Opposite top: The Sydney Cove Overseas Passenger Terminal on the Quay's western shore provides the best 'hotel' location for passengers on the ocean liners that berth here.

Opposite bottom: The ferry wharves at Circular Quay reclaimed 4 hectares (10 acres) of former mud flats. At the head of the cove, the central business district dwarfs Customs House, built in 1840 on the site reputed to be where First Fleet colonists camped in 1788.

Top: Circular Quay is a busy traffic hub for pedestrians. Overhead the Cahill Expressway provides access for cars to and from the Harbour Bridge.

Above: A colonnaded walkway provides shelter for pedestrians walking between the ferry terminals and the Opera House.

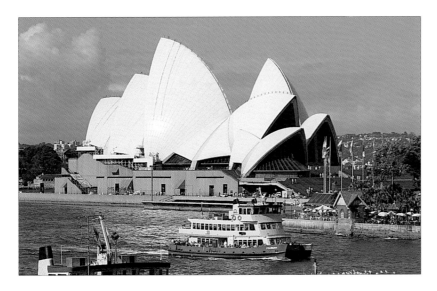

Designed by the imaginative Danish architect Joern Utzon, the Sydney Opera House is probably the world's most outstanding example of 20th-century architecture. As high as a 22-storeyed office building, the multishell-like roof is covered with more than a million tiles. The open ends of the vaults are paned with laminated, amber-coloured glass panels joined by bronze ribs. The podium of the building, hewn from mushroom-pink, reconstituted granite obtained from the Blue Mountains, rests at sea level on a natural sandstone base.

Previous pages: The Harbour Bridge and the Opera House are Australia's most famous icons; this classic Sydney Harbour twilight vista is captured from Mrs Macquarie's Point.
Opposite, above and left: The architectural purity of the Opera House is enhanced by its silhouettes, photographed here at sunset and sunrise. It took over 14 years to complete this revolutionary building which contains five theatre halls, a reception and an exhibition hall, five rehearsal studios, six bars, three restaurants, and almost 1000 rooms. The Opera House engulfs Bennelong Point, named after the Aborigine for whom Governor Arthur Phillip built a house on this same site.

Left: New Year festivities culminate with a spectacular fireworks display staged on the Harbour Bridge, the second most well-known of Sydney's icons. The popular vantage point of Mrs Macquarie's Point on the south side of the Royal Botanic Gardens provides a panorama which also features the Opera House in all its floodlit glory.

Opposite bottom: Bathed in late afternoon light, the Harbour Bridge cuts through The Rocks, the city's oldest urban settlement. The Garrison Church is in the foreground. Heading down to the bridge, Georgian- and Regency-style townhouses and Victorian terraces line Lower Fort Street, which is considered to be one of the city's most notable 19th-century residential streetscapes. Jutting out into Walsh Bay is Pier One, an historic finger wharf which now houses restaurants and shops.

Below: Located on the waterfront at Milsons Point, beside the northwest pylon of the Harbour Bridge, North Sydney Pool enjoys an enviable setting. The Art Deco Olympic-sized pool is a popular venue for staging school swimming competitions, and most of Australia's best-known swimmers, including Olympic gold medallists, honed their talents in these waters.

Opposite: *With room to spare, the replica of the HMAS* Bounty, *built for the film* Mutiny on the Bounty *which stars Mel Gibson, sails under the Harbour Bridge decking, built 52 metres (171 feet) above the high-water line. The original ship captained by the unfortunate Captain Bligh was burnt by Fletcher Christian and his mutineers at Pitcairn Island in 1789. The replica sails from The Rocks daily, taking visitors on popular lunch and dinner cruises.*

Above: *Oblivious to the height, the painters and construction workers employed on the Harbour Bridge head for home down the steel arch which soars 134 metres (440 feet) high. It takes about a decade to paint the bridge and 32 000 litres (56 320 pints) of paint are needed to complete the job.*

Right: *Pedestrians walk across the bridge through archways in the granite pylons which are merely for decoration and not support. Inside the south-east pylon, visitors can climb 200 steps to be rewarded with a superlative vista of Sydney Harbour.*

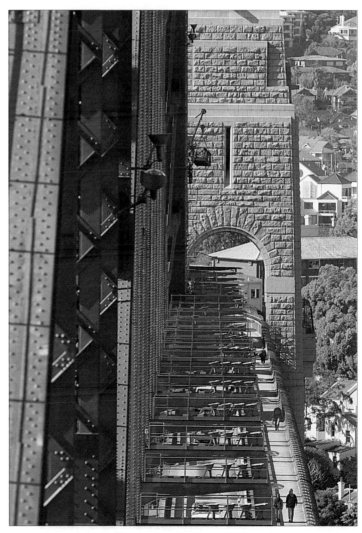

Left: Moored on the western bank of Campbells Cove, tall ships, reminiscent of the golden age of sail, now take visitors on scenic cruises around the harbour. The low-rise Park Hyatt Hotel, built in 1985, curves around the edge of the cove; a pedestrian boardwalk in front leads to Dawes Point. The 18th-century warehouse with the tall chimney has been converted into a Mining and Geological Museum, while the elevated Bradfield Highway on the Harbour Bridge carriageway is named after Dr J. J. Bradfield, the chief railway engineer who designed the bridge in 1911.

Left: Campbell's Warehouse, named after Robert Campbell who first leased the cove in 1798 and owned the warehouse, hosts the popular Waterfront Restaurant where customers dine beside a 19th-century clipper, complete with wooden masts and rigging.

Below: This antique shop sign in Harrington Street harks back to the days when clippers were the only means of exporting goods overseas. The era of sailing ships waned in the 1890s when steam power took over.

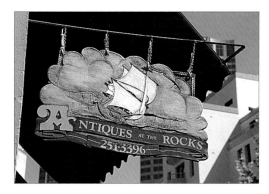

Above: A pillarbox-red hot rod heads along George Street, where 19th-century shophouses contrast with the modern multistoreyed towers.
Left: The striking Dutch Gable House, headquarters of the Australasian Steam Navigation Company and built in 1883, has a viewing platform under the pyramidal tower where company scouts used to look at the harbour.
Below: Playfair Street is fringed with gift shops all the way to The Rocks Square and the Westpac Museum.

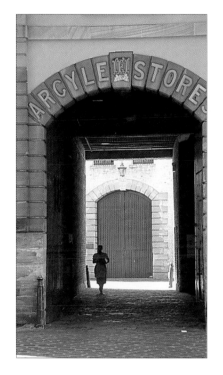

Opposite: On the corner of George Street, Australia's oldest thorough-fare, and Globe Street at the southern end of The Rocks, high-rise hotels and office towers glitter at dusk behind a floodlit 19th-century pub converted into boutiques. It is difficult to imagine that this area was once one of the most notorious port districts in the world and that bubonic plague struck this century with over 100 fatalities.

Above left: On Argyle Street, the key-stone arch bears the original name of the bond stores which now house the Argyle Arts Centre. Building started in 1826 and continued for 60 years. In the converted warehouses overlooking the cobbled courtyard, seen through the arch, are offices, restaurants and shops, while cellars have been hewn from the sandstone bedrock which gives The Rocks its name.

Above and top: The many stylish boutiques and elegant restaurants which abound along the northern end of George Street are evidence of the reconstruction of The Rocks into an area of upmarket dining. With the growing popularity of inner-city living, some of Sydney's most prominent chefs and successful restaurant entrepreneurs have relocated to this area.

Previous pages: Darling Harbour has been transformed from an old maritime cove into a hub of shops, restaurants, museums, and open pedestrian malls.

Opposite: The wave-shaped Sydney Aquarium on the city side of Darling Harbour is dwarfed by late-20th-century skyscrapers.

Above: Pyrmont Bridge, built at the turn of the century, provides the foot link between the city and Darling Harbour.

Top right: The South Steyne, a much loved ferry that used to travel between Manly and Circular Quay, now serves as an Olympic Showcase and Information Centre.

Right: The glass-roofed entrance archway to Darling Harbour's Harbourside Festival Marketplace creates a striking overhead frame.

Above and opposite, top right:
The National Maritime Museum at Darling Harbour, designed by the eminent Sydney architect Philip Cox, utilises a nautical theme in keeping with the thousands of exhibits ranging from Aboriginal fishing techniques and life on the convict ships to the evolution of surfboards and the history of the bikini. Ships on display in the 10-storeyed museum include a World War II commando boat, a pearling lugger from Broome in Western Australia, a Vietnamese refugee boat which completed the journey through the South China Sea to Australia, and a racing cutter from 1888.
Right: The monorail offers great views of the museum as it snakes across Pyrmont Bridge to Darling Harbour. It then travels on to Chinatown and completes its circuit around the lower part of the city.

Below: *The largest exhibit is the
HMAS* Vampire, *the former Royal
Australian Navy destroyer, which
provides an insightful look at what
it was like to live and work on the
last of the big gun ships.*

Bottom: *Passengers alight from the
monorail at the Harbourside Station
for the National Maritime Museum
and the nearby markets.*

Previous pages: At the Sydney Aquarium beside the Darling Harbour ferry wharf, architect Philip Cox came up with the novel idea of submerging the fish tanks in the harbour. This not only reduced costs by balancing the water pressure, it also provided visitors with the unique experience of an underwater descent. In the Open Ocean exhibit, onlookers can walk through the 146 metres (160 yards) of underwater tunnels and are surrounded by one of the world's largest collections of sharks. Other marine creatures on display here include Australia's notorious crocodiles, dolphins, and thousands of native fish species.

Left: Chinese lions guard the entrance archway of Dixon Street, the hub of Sydney's Chinatown which dates from the early 19th century. The columns are coloured red to symbolise happiness and prosperity, and the gold calligraphy means 'Understanding, Virtue and Trust'.

Below: At the adjacent Chinese Gardens, the largest Cantonese gardens outside China, a waterside pavilion surrounded by willows provides a peaceful contrast to the bustle of the nearby city. These gardens were designed by Chinese landscape architects from the Guandong Province and they symbolise the links between China and Australia.

Opposite, top: *Trees arch peacefully over the Avenue of Remembrance in Hyde Park, providing a shaded retreat on hot summer days.*

Opposite, bottom left: *Onlookers ponder the next chess move at the park's outdoor chess venue.*

Opposite, bottom right: *The Art Deco-style Anzac War Memorial at the southern end of Hyde Park was built in 1934 and is dedicated to the Anzacs – the Australian and New Zealand Army Corps who fought together during World War I.*

Above: *Symbolising the nation's youthful future, a statue of Apollo points the way atop the Archibald Fountain in the northern precinct of Hyde Park. Built in 1932 to commemorate the friendship between France and Australia during World War I, the fountain was financed by its namesake, Jules Francois Archibald, who was a leading Sydney publisher and journalist.*

Top right: *Visitors take a break beside the Archibald Fountain.*

Above right: *Aboriginal motifs decorate this fountain at the Sandringham Gardens near the corner of Park and College Streets.*

Right: *Named after its London counterpart, Hyde Park was fenced during Governor Macquarie's term of office in 1810 and was originally much larger. Bordered by Elizabeth, Liverpool and College streets, with St James Road to the north, the park is a favourite lunch-time rendezvous for office workers. The colony's first horse races were held here and around its perimeter are many historic buildings.*

Left: *Sydney Tower soars above the central business district, bordered to the east by the green lungs of Hyde Park and the Royal Botanic Gardens. East of the Gardens is Woolloomooloo Bay with its historic finger wharf, and the naval dockyards of Garden Island. Woolloomooloo, thought to derive from the Aboriginal word for 'young kangaroo', was the scene of fierce resident, conservationist and union protests during the 1970s when the area was slated for massive redevelopment. The protests were very successful and Woolloomooloo was allowed to retain many of its historic residential areas.*

Above: *The monorail passes through the central city section of its circular route. Sydney Tower and the high-rise offices of Market Street can be seen in the background.*

Opposite, top and bottom: *Built in 1906, Central Railway Station is considered an architectural marvel of that time. It was the first Australian building to use reinforced concrete. Natural light filters through the roof in the great hall, which is still the arrival and departure nucleus of the state's rail system.*

Above: *The University of Sydney, Australia's oldest tertiary institution, was built in 1854 and echoes the Gothic Revival style of both Oxford and Cambridge. The original buildings are now surrounded by more modern buildings due to the expansion of campus needs.*

Right: *Also built in Gothic Revival style, the construction of St Mary's Roman Catholic Cathedral took from 1868 to 1928. It is the world's sixth-largest cathedral.*

Above: *The Museum of Contemporary Art at Circular Quay originally functioned as the offices of the Maritime Services Board which controlled harbour shipping. Works by contemporary Australian and international artists are displayed here.*
Right: *A busker entertains the passers-by on the waterfront at Circular Quay with his bushman instruments – a saw, which suffices as a fiddle, and a gum-leaf whistle.*

Right: *The Powerhouse takes its name from its original use as the power house for the old trams that used to run along Sydney's streets. It is now Australia's largest museum, a branch of the Museum of Applied Arts and Sciences. The fascinating 'hands-on' exhibits take visitors on a journey through the past and future of science, technology and the arts. The Powerhouse is reputed to be one of the world's great museums.*

Below: *The Mint Museum building was originally part of Sydney's first hospital, the Rum Hospital built in 1816. It became the mint in 1853, following the gold rush. The attractive two-storeyed verandah is supported by cedar columns.*

Left: Sydney's city centre, like this streetscape in Pitt Street, shows a range of architectural styles from Victorian to late-20th-century post-modern. The old corner pub is flanked by the 40-storeyed tower of the glass-walled Gateway Plaza.

Top: This mushroom-shaped building in Martin Place, the state's financial centre, houses the Commercial Travellers Club, and office workers take advantage of the spacious steps to catch some sunlight, a rarity in Martin Place as it is usually shaded by skyscrapers.

Above: The Skygarden retail centre in Pitt Street Mall, a paved pedestrian block between King and Market streets in the heart of the commercial centre, contains six levels of retail pleasure and an international food court.

Left: *Straddling an entire city block and bordered by George, Druitt, York and Market streets, the Queen Victoria Building (popularly known as the QVB), built in 1883, was boarded up and under threat of demolition for decades. It underwent a multimillion-dollar refurbishment and reopened as a speciality shopping centre in 1986.*
Below left: *A larger-than-life statue of the building's namesake, Queen Victoria, presides over the urban throng at the Druitt Street entrance.*
Below: *Twenty-one copper-sheathed domes, the largest being 20 metres (66 feet) in diameter, crown this ornamental building which once served as the city's municipal markets.*
Right: *A glass barrel vault skylight provides natural lighting in the three-storeyed shopping arcade where the QVB's Royal Clock is suspended from the ceiling.*

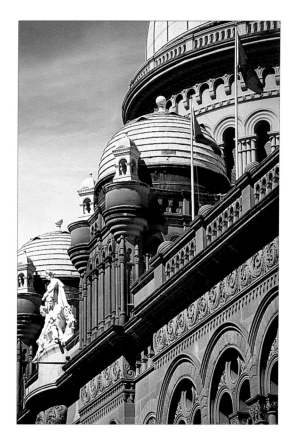

Left: *Australia Day celebrations held every year on 26 January maintain a link with the day in 1770 when Captain Arthur Phillip, commander of the First Fleet of convict transports, set up camp on the shores of Sydney Cove and raised the British flag on the colony of New South Wales. The annual ferry race in Sydney Harbour is a colourful highlight of the celebration.*

Below: *The sail-past on Australia Day consists of clippers and ketches, tall ships of a bygone age, all of which parade past the shark-nosed shells of the Opera House, under the Harbour Bridge and into Darling Harbour. Sightseers flock to the foreshores of the harbour to watch the festive spectacle.*

90

Above: Buskers entertain the Australia Day crowd along the paved walkway around Sydney Cove. Often there are different acts going on all around the area: an Irish fiddler, an American juggling flaming torches, an Aborigine on a didgeridoo, Andean musicians, mimes, magicians, and hawkers selling toys.

Left: An essential prop for most street parades on this day is the Australian flag. The Union Jack in the corner is a heritage from British rule and the stars represent the Southern Cross, the major star constellation of the Southern Hemisphere.

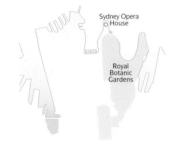

Sydney Opera House

Royal Botanic Gardens

Opposite: *The Royal Botanic Gardens are beautifully situated. Wrapping around Farm Cove, the mown lawns, mature fig trees, duck ponds, whimsical marble statues* **(above right)**, *and theme gardens – like the palm forest with the world's largest collection of palms, and the rainforest in a glass pyramid – make a visit to the Gardens memorable.*

Above: *Victorian statuary abounds in the Gardens, but this monument is unusual. A copy of the Chorago Monument of Lysicrates in Athens, it was built in 1870 when the classical architecture of Ancient Greece was making a worldwide revival.*

Above: For over two centuries ferry services have provided a thriving waterway link between the city and the suburbs. Circular Quay has been the harbour's ferry terminus since Sydney's earliest days. Services head across the water to foreshore suburbs like Mosman and Cremorne, and Taronga Park Zoo, down the harbour to Manly and the eastern bays like Watsons Bay, and up to historic Balmain.

Right: Dinner cruises at dusk are a popular way to enjoy the night lights of Sydney Harbour, while the daytime panoramas make it obvious why a trip on a Sydney ferry is a must for all visitors.

Right and below: *A worthy addition to Sydney's architectural icons of the Opera House and Harbour Bridge is Stadium Australia. Purpose built as the main venue for the 2000 Olympic Games, the stadium boasts state-of-the-art environmental features and has been designed specifically for the Australian climate, providing plenty of shade for spectators. As the largest outdoor venue in Olympic history, the stadium is capable of seating 110 000, and was built at a cost of A$690 million.*

THE SUBURBS

Opposite: Harbour-frontage homes in exclusive Birchgrove.
Above: Victorian-era terrace houses in Paddington.

Engulfing an area six times the size of Rome and numbering almost a thousand, Sydney's suburbs stretch 60 kilometres (37 miles) from north to south along the Pacific coastline and almost the same distance from the city to the foot of the Blue Mountains in the west. Dozens of suburbs boast a harbour frontage where marinas are more numerous than car parks – the reason for Sydneysiders' yachting prowess – and dozens more have harbour views – the reason why the city's real estate is Australia's highest priced.

At least 30 suburbs fringe some of the world's best beaches, including famed Bondi – the closest, and most accessible, to the city centre – which accounts for Sydneysiders' passion for sand and surf. Vast national parks of eucalyptus forests, heathlands and rainforested gullies back up to many of the northern and southern suburbs, providing miles of bush walks through original natural landscapes where rock engravings of Sydney's Aboriginal inhabitants can still be found. Inner-city suburbs like Paddington, Balmain and Glebe are famed for their Victorian-style terrace houses, art galleries, street markets, and cafe scene; Kings Cross for its nightlife ranging from sleazy clubs to chic restaurants; Ultimo for its museums; Haymarket for its bustling Chinatown; and Darlinghurst for its annual Gay and Lesbian Mardi Gras.

Overlooking the harbour are wealthy suburbs such as Double Bay with its designer boutiques and millionaires' mansions, Hunters Hill with its century-old ivy-clad residences, Cremorne with its harbourside parks and wonderful views, and Manly with its beachside promenade and famous ferry journey to and from the city. West of the city is the former industrial suburb of Homebush which has been transformed into the sporting hub of the 2000 Olympics; Cabramatta, Australia's most Asian suburb where it is rare to hear English spoken in the streets and common to experience culinary delights; West Pennant Hills, the home of Koala Park Sanctuary, Sydney's best-known koala reserve; and Parramatta, the capital of the western suburbs and the second-oldest settlement in Australia.

Opposite, top: *Notorious Kings Cross is the centre of Sydney's nightlife. At the top of William Street a giant billboard depicting the world's best-known advertising icon marks the entrance to Darlinghurst Road.*
Opposite, bottom: *This neon hub is where adults-only clubs shoulder pawn shops and fast-food joints.*
Top: *Bistros, like the Bourbon and Beefsteak, opened in the 1960s when US servicemen on leave from the Vietnam War came to Sydney.*

Above left: *Kings Cross is a favourite spot for local biker gangs who line their 'hardware' along any available parking space in the road.*
Top and above: *Mounted police lend a peaceful air to the tree-lined streets where old apartment buildings now cater for backpackers drawn to the area for its 24-hour lifestyle and after-hours money exchanges.*

Hedonists of all sexual persuasions turn out in force for the colourful Sydney Gay and Lesbian Mardi Gras held annually in March. The city's most flamboyant and outrageous parade attracts over half a million spectators, and onlookers jam every available vantage point along the Darlinghurst end of Oxford Street. This is the heart of Sydney's gay community. The Mardi Gras began as a political protest march in 1978. Arrests made at that march highlighted the gay cause, and when the charges were dropped, the campaigners claimed a moral victory. They decided to stage a parade every year as a reminder of their struggle for equal rights and recognition. It is now a permanent fixture on Sydney's events calendar and is the highlight of the month-long Gay and Lesbian Mardi Gras Festival.

Paddington, considered one of the
world's best-preserved Victorian-era
suburbs, is a maze of steep hillside
roads lined with superbly restored
terrace houses, interspersed with art
galleries, bookshops, cafes and pubs.

Building began around Paddington
in the early colonial days but the
boom came in the 1880s when the
entire suburb was subdivided for
terrace houses, most of which still
survive today. The area has had a
chequered history. It began as an
upper-middle-class area, then fell
from favour when the new outer
suburbs attracted city dwellers to
the larger 'quarter-acre' blocks.

During the inter-war years
Paddington was considered a slum,
but after the area was settled and
reinvigorated by Mediterranean
immigrants in the 1950s, the

younger middle classes discovered the joys and convenience of inner-city living in the 1960s and Paddington never looked back.

Above and top right: Neighbourhood pubs, like the London Tavern on William Street and the Royal Hotel at Five Ways, have seen their clientele change from tough razor gangs and beer-swilling labourers in the 1930s to today's yuppies with their mobile phones and designer jeans.

Opposite, bottom: Paddington Markets, which began in 1973, is the best place to shop for all kinds of weird and wonderful goodies.

Opposite, top: The markets also have a reputation for attracting a spectrum of bizarre characters.

Right: Today the terrace houses of Paddington are among the most sought after in Sydney.

Above, left, and opposite, top:
Centennial Park provides a huge open space at the south end of Oxford Street in Paddington and, as its name suggests, dates from Australia's centenary celebrations of 1888. The then state premier declared the area 'the people's park', a title which is as apt today as it was then. Joggers, cyclers, horse-riders, picnickers and residents who need a break from urban stress are fiercely protective of their park and have opposed all developments. The ashes of the most famous campaigner and nearby resident, Patrick White, a Nobel prize-winning author, were scattered around his beloved Centennial Park.

Below: Randwick Racecourse west of Centennial Park is the best-known of Sydney's five suburban horse-racing venues. Sydney's first recorded horse race took place in Hyde Park in 1810 and was a success from the very beginning. In 1860 the Australian Jockey Club (AJC) began holding its meetings at Randwick, which is still the home of the AJC today.

Right and below: Sydney's most exclusive real estate is found in the bays and coves of the eastern suburbs. Bristling with yacht masts, the marinas of Rushcutters Bay are a far cry from the early colonial days when convicts came to the swamps behind the bay to cut rushes for thatching.

Opposite: Darling Point to the east of the bay is home to luxury harbourside residences and high-rise apartments that command Australia's highest prices. Some of the original estates, Georgian mansions surrounded by mature trees, still survive on the tip of the point.

Left: *Luxurious mansions and apartments crowd the promontory of Point Piper, situated between Double Bay and Rose Bay. Lady Martins Beach, within the small Felix Bay at the end of the point, is one of Australia's most exclusive beaches. Clarke Island, situated just off Darling Point, is one of three islands that form part of the Sydney Harbour National Park. Boats regularly depart from the many marinas in the eastern suburbs to take picnickers to this uninhabited haven.*
Below and bottom: *Beyond Darling Point is Double Bay where chic sidewalk cafes and exclusive boutiques line the streets of this harbourside enclave.*

Opposite, top: North of Rose Bay, towards the South Head, is the exclusive suburb of Vaucluse where the Gothic-style Vaucluse House is located. The original house was built in 1803 but it was extensively renovated by William Charles Wentworth in the 1830s. Wentworth was one of the explorers who first crossed the Blue Mountains and is also sometimes referred to as the 'father of the Australian Constitution'. It is reputed that the house was the site for the first cabinet meeting of the newly enfranchised New South Wales government in 1856.

Opposite, bottom: On the foreshores of the bay, local youths learn from an early age the ways of the water in small, one-man sailboats.

Above: Perched on the eastern hill overlooking Rose Bay, a picturesque foreshore suburb of Sydney, is the prominent Sacred Heart Convent, a Roman Catholic college. The chapel of this college was designed by the eccentric architect John Horbury Hunt, who died a pauper in 1904 after losing his entire fortune in the 1890s depression.

Opposite and below: *Watsons Bay enjoys a unique location at the eastern extremity of the city. The bay still retains a fishing village atmosphere: boats pulled up on the shore are reminders of the old days when fishermen hauled their catch onto the beach where, from 1792, a fishery operated. Watsons Bay is famed for its tranquil waters, parks, walking trails, and its seafood dining. To the north, beyond Laings Point, is Camp Cove, a popular swimming beach.*
Left: *Australia's best-known seafood eatery, Doyles Restaurant, is located beside Fishermans Wharf at Watsons Bay. It is still run by the descendants of the same fishing family who started the business in 1885. Diners not only enjoy wonderful seafood but also the 'spot', as the original owner called this location, which has an unsurpassed view of harbour and city.*

Above: Onlookers crowd the clifftops at South Head, and spectator and media craft flank the yachts as they move to the start of the annual Sydney to Hobart Yacht Race. The race, held every Boxing Day, began as an outing in 1945 for the members of the Cruising Yacht Club of Australia.

Opposite, top: The Gap bluff is on the eastern side of South Head peninsula and is part of the Sydney Harbour National Park. The dramatic vertical cliffs of The Gap, plunging to a rock platform and heaving seas below, have the dubious distinction of being Sydney's favourite venue for suicides.

Opposite bottom: Macquarie Lighthouse was the first major work to be designed in the colony by the convict architect Francis Greenway. The lighthouse was such a success that Greenway was awarded a conditional pardon from the governor on its completion.

Previous pages and left: On a sparkling summer's day it is easy to see why Bondi Beach has earned such an international reputation. The sweep of sand lies between Ben Buckler and Mackenzies Point. Perched high upon Ben Buckler clifftop is the Bondi golf course which must rate at the top of the register as one of the world's most spectacular golfing locations.

Top: Surf-lifesavers are a common sight on Sydney's beaches. These days they punch through the surf in motorised rubber dinghies rather than the original wooden surfboats that were in use when the Surf Life Saving Association of Australia was first formed in 1907.

Right: Bondi attracts a diverse and cosmopolitan crowd and is also popular with rollerbladers and skateboarders who delight the crowds with their skills on a specially built concrete ramp in Bondi Park which fronts the beach.

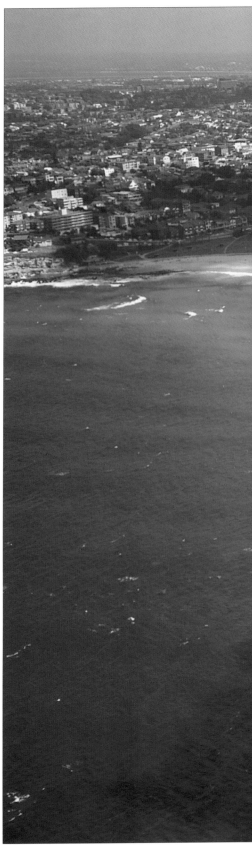

Right: *Situated to the south of Bondi Beach, Marks Park crowns Mackenzies Point, and further around the headland are the sheltered beaches of Tamarama Bay and Bronte.*

Top: *The name 'Tamarama' is a distortion of the original Aboriginal word for the bay which appeared on an 1860s map as 'Gamma Gamma'.*
Above: *Bronte takes its name from the first estate in the area, which was named after the Duke of Bronte by the owner of the estate in the mid-1800s.*

Above: Further south, Coogee, once a family suburb, has become fashionable for young city professionals. Seawater pools line the southern foreshore of Coogee Beach beside the Coogee Surf Life Saving Club. The foreshore has been enlivened with cafes that have adventurous menus, and the backpacker crowd flocks here for cheap beachside hostels.

Left: The foreshore areas of the La Perouse and Kurnell peninsulas comprise the Botany Bay National Park and mark the entrance to Botany Bay. The stretch of coastline to the north of Botany Bay looks very much the same today as it did all those years ago when Captain Cook first spied it in 1770.

Opposite, top: On the La Perouse side of the bay, a footbridge goes to Bare Island where a fort, which protected the area in the 19th century, has been converted into a museum.

Below: No less than four golf courses occupy the area of land adjacent to the Botany Bay National Park near La Perouse. Winds coming from the ocean and the bay make conditions during a game of golf at the 6232-metre-long (6815-yard) New South Wales Golf Course reminiscent of a game at Scotland's St Andrews Golf Course.

Below: The Macquarie Watchtower, built in 1820, overlooks Botany Bay's entrance, and it was also once used as a lookout for checking on the activities of smugglers.

Previous pages: *The lower North Shore suburbs are peppered with parklands, beaches, inlets and coves. The headlands jutting into the harbour include the suburbs of Neutral Bay in the foreground, followed by Cremorne where a walkway around Cremorne Point affords wonderful views. Beyond Cremorne is Mosman Bay and the wooded hills of Taronga Park Zoo.*

Taronga Park Zoo opened on the foreshore at the end of Bradleys Head Road in Mosman in 1916, and took in all the animals from the previous zoo that had been located at Moore Park since 1881.

Opposite, top left and top right: *Animals from all over the world, including giraffes and elephants, have been introduced to the zoo. The first ferry from Circular Quay to the zoo in 1916 carried an elephant named Jessie to her new home. The animal enclosures have been designed to reflect the natural habitats, like a simulated rainforest which houses the Orang-utans. There is a Koala Walkabout where visitors can view these marsupials from an elevated walkway, and the platypus exhibit offers the opportunity to watch this rarely seen creature swimming and frolicking in a glass-enclosed tank.*

Opposite, bottom: *The name 'Taronga' comes from the Aboriginal word for 'spectacular harbour view'; it is not difficult to understand why it was quickly adopted.*

Below: *The copper-domed entrance pavilion dates from the zoo's inception.*

Left: The Spit, named after the sand spit which juts into Middle Harbour, is flanked by marinas housing yachts and cruisers. The Spit Road across the bridge leads to the northern beaches. At various times during the day, the bridge spans are raised to allow boats and ferries to travel further into Middle Harbour.

Below: Clontarf to the east of Spit Bridge is named after a waterfront Dublin suburb. Clontarf made headlines in 1868 when an assassination attempt was made on the then Duke of Edinburgh by an Irish extremist.

Bottom: Chinamans Beach to the south of The Spit was named after an 1890s Chinese market garden.

Previous pages, below right and bottom: Manly's superb location between the ocean and the harbour is the reason why it has been such a popular suburb ever since the 1850s when an English-born entrepreneur realised its potential. 'It is truly delightful', he wrote, 'there is nothing like it in the wide, wide world'. The stretch of ocean shoreline actually comprises three beaches – Queenscliff to the north, North Steyne and Manly to the south – and is renowned for its excellent surf and golden sands. These days topless bathing is considered normal yet in 1902 a local newspaper editor was arrested for swimming in daylight. He launched an appeal against the curfew and swimmers have flocked to Manly ever since.

Below left: The Corso, Manly's most famous thoroughfare which links the ocean beach to Manly Cove, has a beach resort atmosphere.

Opposite top: At Manly Cove the underwater tunnel at Ocean World is where you can come face to face with sharks and giant stingrays. During the daily feeding session, divers handfeed these giants of the deep.

Left: *A statue of Duke Kahanamoku, Hawaiian Olympic gold-medallist of the 1912 Olympic Games, stands on the north point of Freshwater Beach to commemorate his exhibition of surfboard riding at this beach in 1915. This display marked the beginning of one of Australia's most popular sports.*

Opposite bottom: *Beyond Freshwater are the Rock Baths which stand at the southern end of Curl Curl Beach. The name Curl Curl comes from the winding lagoon behind the cliffs at Dee Why Head* **(above)**, *where luxury homes complete with swimming pools perch precariously above the pounding surf.*

Right: *Seagulls peck around the shallows at Dee Why Beach further to the north, another example of the superb array of Sydney's beaches.*

135

Above: The expansive white sands of Long Reef sweep to the north from Dee Why Beach. Long Reef, a favourite venue for surfers, gets really spectacular surf when heavy seas create waves at the bombora, a submerged reef. Long Reef Golf Course straddles the promontory behind the beach.

Left: A paraglider soars above the Long Reef Aquatic Reserve which is situated at the northern end of Long Reef Beach.

Right: *Warriewood Beach is just north of rocky Turimetta Head and is backed by a recreation reserve. This idyllic spot is a favourite for surfers as the breakers hit the headland and move towards the sand. Just north of Warriewood is Mona Vale where the Mona Vale (Beeby Park) Golf Course meets the sand and affords fabulous views of the ocean for the players.*
Below: *The Northern Beaches run along the ocean side of a long peninsula and on the other side is the fabulous Pittwater. Heron Cove, on the Pittwater, is virtually parallel to Newport Beach; the cove is often used by rowers because the calm waters are ideal for their practice and racing meets.*

Left: *From Mona Vale to the top of the northern beaches peninsula the major road is called Barrenjoey, after the headland that forms the tip of the peninsula. The road sweeps over the hilltops, offering lovely views, and in parts runs very close to the beaches. Newport Beach is separated from the road only by the narrow Eric Green reserve and is a peaceful beach favoured by the locals.*

Below: *Just around the corner from Newport is Bilgola Beach. Smaller by comparison, the beach lies at the bottom of the Bilgola Plateau where the Avalon Golf Course is perched. A rock bath has been created at the southern end near the surf club house. All the northern beaches have a relaxed lifestyle, which is why they are popular among Sidneysiders.*

Opposite, top: *Whale Beach is one of Sydney's northernmost beaches and is a particular favourite with surfboard riders.*

Opposite, bottom: *At the very end of the long stretch of northern beaches is Shark Point, part of the Ku-ring-gai Chase National Park. Shark Point is on the inside of the headland at the entrance to Broken Bay. On the ocean side is Barrenjoey Head.*

Left: Lion Island, crouching like its namesake in the mouth of Broken Bay where the Hawkesbury River meets the Pacific Ocean, is a familiar sight for sailors on Pittwater. This expansive inlet, named by Governor Phillip in Sydney's founding year, laps around the back of the far northern beaches, known collectively as 'the Peninsula'.

Above: Brooklyn, a favourite stop-over for cruises on the Hawkesbury River, is the starting place for the unusual 'Riverboat Postman' cruise which follows the trail of Australia's last riverboat mailman.

Following pages: Sydney's northern barrier, the Ku-ring-gai Chase National Park, is a spectacular region of flooded river valleys. Like Smith's Creek, it is the result of the ice age around 6 million years ago.

OUTSIDE SYDNEY

Opposite: The Jenolan Caves lie within a bushland setting.
Above: The quaint gallery in the Kangaroo Valley.

Mountain resorts, endless beaches, vast national parks, world-famous vineyards, historical towns, wonderful waterways for cruising and fishing, and beautiful rural scenery are just a part of the wealth of attractions on offer within a day's drive from Sydney. To the west of the city are the box canyons of the Blue Mountains, famed for incomparable views, bush walks through a 200 000-hectare (494 200-acre) national park, sheer cliffs which are an abseiler's delight, olde-worlde retreats with renowned spring and autumn gardens, and the cave system at Jenolan which includes Australia's largest open cave. Travel south down the Princes Highway, along the shores of the Pacific and past the Royal National Park (the nation's oldest and famous for its unspoilt beaches and spring wildflowers) to Stanwell Tops, where the mountains meet the sea. The highway winds around some of Australia's most spectacular scenery, past some excellent surfing beaches and old coal-mining villages to Wollongong – the Steel City – and onwards to the picturesque fishing port of Kiama and the historical town of Berry. Further on are dairy farms with green rolling farmlands, and the rainforests of Minnamurra. Climb the escarpment to the Southern Highlands where early settlers, lured by the cooler climate, transformed the countryside into European farmlands and built towns which still have a distinctly English ambience, among them Bowral, famed for its tulip festival, and neighbouring Moss Vale.

North of Sydney the highway cleaves the flooded valleys of the rugged Ku-ring-gai Chase National Park, crosses the Hawkesbury River – a favourite for river cruisers – to the capital of the Central Coast, Gosford which has long been the favourite weekend destination of Sydneysiders. Lakelands renowned for their good fishing and excellent surfing and swimming beaches intersect the coastline to Newcastle, the second-largest city of New South Wales, and dubbed 'the Coal City' for its biggest industry. Only a short drive inland, Australia's famous vineyards nestle in the Hunter Valley and produce some of the country's best wines.

Above: *Evans Lookout at Blackheath, 1064 metres (3491 feet) above sea level, overlooks the canyons of the Grose Valley in the Blue Mountains National Park about 108 kilometres (67 miles) west of Sydney.*
Left: *Early 20th-century shopfronts line the main street in Katoomba, the 'capital' of the Blue Mountains which has always attracted a steady stream of sightseers ever since the region was touted in the late 1800s as a health resort.*

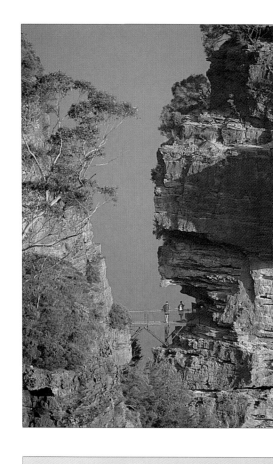

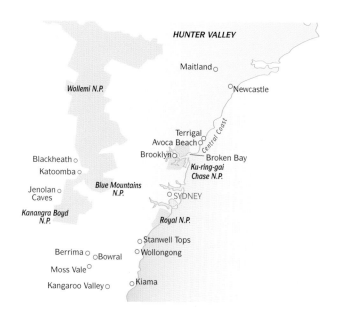

HUNTER VALLEY

Maitland

Newcastle

Wollemi N.P.

Central Coast

Terrigal
Avoca Beach
Brooklyn — Broken Bay
Blackheath
Ku-ring-gai
Chase N.P.
Katoomba
Blue Mountains
N.P.
Jenolan
Caves
SYDNEY
Kanangra Boyd
N.P.
Royal N.P.

Stanwell Tops
Berrima   Bowral
Wollongong
Moss Vale
Kangaroo Valley   Kiama

Left and below: *Katoomba's most photographed attraction is the Three Sisters, rocky tors overlooking the Jamison Valley. Views from a suspended walkway are not for the faint-hearted. Bushwalkers can descend to the valley floor and follow a scenic trail through rainforest and eucalypts to the base station of the Scenic Railway.*

Above and right: In the Southern Highlands town of Bowral, famed as a country retreat for Sydneysiders, heritage buildings are a tangible reminder of the area's European history which began around 1815. Bowral's biggest tourist attraction is the annual tulip festival centred on the town's Corbett Gardens.

Opposite, top and bottom right: The grand former post office at Berry, an old agricultural town on the South Coast between Wollongong and Nowra, is now a coffee shop, while other 19th-century buildings have been revamped as guesthouses, restaurants and craft shops.

Opposite, bottom left: Berrima, the most historic town of the Southern Highlands, was bypassed by the railway in the 1860s and when businesses moved to Bowral, the town stayed just as it was. This colonial township from the Georgian era is today listed by the National Trust.

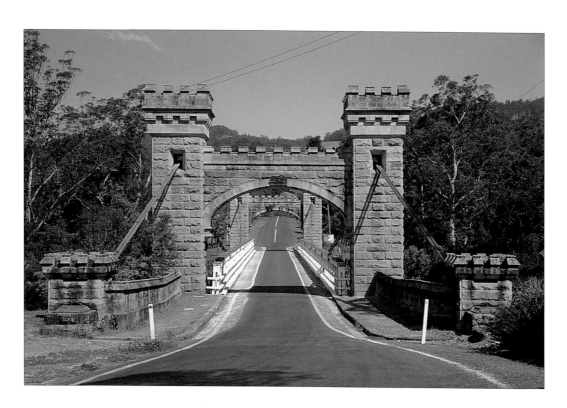

Opposite: *Kangaroo Valley, tucked between the mountains and the sea, consists of a number of fertile valleys and historic homes on the South Coast.*

Above: *Built in 1898 in the style of a medieval castle, the incongruous Hampden Bridge on the South Coast in Kangaroo Valley looks rather out of place in this peaceful rural spot.*

Right: *Beside the road from Kangaroo Valley to Moss Vale, the Fitzroy Falls plunge 81 metres (266 feet) from the top of the escarpment to the rainforest below. Walking trails winding around the top of the cliffs provide stunning vistas of these and other waterfalls in this scenic corner of Morton National Park.*

Opposite, top and bottom:
Wollongong, the third-largest city of
New South Wales, is situated on a
narrow coastal plain backed by the
Illawarra Escarpment. The city owes
its existence to the steelworks at
nearby Port Kembla, but despite its
industrial reputation the area boasts
wonderful beaches, parklands, a
university, shopping malls and
a picturesque harbour.

Above left: From the top of the cliffs
at Stanwell Tops, just south of the
Royal National Park, the view down
the coast to where the mountains
meet the sea is one of the most
remarkable vistas of the South Coast.

Above: Jutting out into the ocean at
the southern end of the Wollongong
Harbour is Flagstaff Point where two
lighthouses are perched. The cannons
surrounding the lighthouse are relics
of the colonial era.

Left: The Royal National Park has
survived almost unchanged since the
arrival of the Europeans. Beautiful
bays, beaches, cliffs, woodlands and
heaths lie protected within its borders.

Above: In the Broken Bay region, near the mouth of the Hawkesbury River, there are many marinas and mooring facilities. Several boating sheds, like this one at Brooklyn, offer boats for hire – the perfect way to explore the Hawkesbury basin.

Left: The resort town of Avoca lies between a lake and a beach of the same name. The region has a relaxed and unpretentious ambience and over the years it has become a favourite holiday and retirement spot.

Opposite: The southern end of Terrigal Beach, north of Avoca and only a short bus ride from Gosford, is protected by a rocky bluff known as the Skillion. The lagoon behind the beach is a good spot for fishing and swimming. The whole Central Coast has experienced a boom in the tourist trade because of the wonderful water sports on offer and its close proximity to the Tuggerah Lake district.

Above and Right: *Renowned vineyards and guesthouses like the award-winning Peppers in the Hunter Valley are popular destinations for city dwellers yearning for a weekend retreat. The Hunter Valley is one of Australia's best-known wine-growing regions; vines have been grown here since 1858.*

Page references in *italic* refer to photographs.

A

Abbotsford 40
Aboriginal
    art *16*, 17, 18, 26, 47, 97
    culture 15, 18, 20
    Dreamtime 15, 16, 19
    place names 17
Aborigines 11, 13, 15, 16, *17*, *19*, 42
Adams, George 34
Admiralty House *28*, 29
Albion Park 45
Allen, George 40
Andrews, Graeme 30
Anzac War Memorial 34, *78*
Archibald
    Fountain 34, *79*
    Jules 34, *79*
architecture 33
Argyle
    Arts Centre *67*
    Cut 23
    Place 23
    Street 22, *67*
Art Gallery of New South
    Wales 26
Australia Day 20, *90*, *91*
Australian Museum 34
Avalon 38
Avenue of Remembrance 34, *78*
Avoca Beach 47, *154*

B

Bald Hill 45
Balmain 29, 40, 94, 97
    William 40
Bare Island *123*
Barnet, James 24, 25, 35, 38
Barracks Cafe 25
Barrallier
    Falls 42
    Francis 42
Barrenjoey 16, 17, 38, 138
Basin, the 38
Baths, the (Bondi Beach) *36*
Bayview 38
Ben Buckler 119
Bennelong Point 25, 59
Berkeley 46
Berrima 44, *149*
Berry 45, 46, *149*
    Alexander 46
Bicentenary Park 41
Bilgola Beach 38, *138*
Birchgrove *96*
Bishopscourt 33

Black Sunday 36
Blacket, Edmund 40
Blackheath 43, 146
Blackwattle Bay 40
Blaxland 43
    Gregory 42
Bligh, William 23, 63
Blue Mountains 11, 15, 33, 38, 42, 43, 54, 97, 111, 145, 146
    National Park *42*, *146*
Bondi
    Beach 17, 33, *35*, 36, 97, *116–117*, *118*, *119*, 120
    Iceberg Club 36
    Park *119*
Botany Bay 16, 17, *19*, 20, 36, 37, 122
    National Park *122*, 123
Bouddi National Park 47
Bourke Street 31
Bowral 44, 145, *148*
Boyd, Arthur 45
Bradfield
    Dr J. J. 27, 64
    Highway 21, *64*
Bradley, William 16
Bradleys Head 16, 30
    Road 127
Bradman
    Donald 44
    Museum 44
Bridge Street 24
Brisbane Water National
    Park 47
Broadway 34, 39
Broken Bay 18, 20, 38, 138, 141, 154
Bronte Beach 36, *120*
Brooklyn 46, *141*, *154*
Bulli
    Lookout 45
    Pass 46
Bundanoon 45
Bungan Beach 38
Burrawang 45
bushfires 16, 18
bushwalking 43
Busker's End 44

C

Cabramatta 14, 97
Cadman, John 21
Cahill Expressway 25, 26, *53*
Cambewarra Mountain 46
Camp Cove *113*
Campbells Cove *21*, 22, *64*
Campbell's Warehouse *64*
Campbell, Robert 64
Capon, Edmund 28

casino 40
Caves House 43
Centennial Park 32, *104*, *105*
Central Coast 38, 46, 47, 145, 154
Central Railway Station 39, *82*
Centrepoint Arcade 35
Cessnock 47
Chief Secretary's Building 24
Chinamans Beach *129*
Chinatown 13, 14, *39*, 72, *76*, 97
Chinese
    Garden 39, *77*
    Opera *13*
Christian, Fletcher 63
Church Point 38
Circular Quay 20, 21, 22, 23, 28, 29, 35, 40, 49, *50–51*, *52*, 71, 84, 94, 127
City to Surf Run 33
Clareville 38
Clarke
    Island 109
    Marcus 20
Clifton Gardens 18
climate 12
Clontarf *129*
Clovelly 36
Coalcliff 45
Coaldale 45
cockatoos 19
Cockle Bay 38
Collaroy 38
College Street 34, *79*
Colonial Mutual Life
    Building 35
Commercial Travellers Club *87*
Conservatorium of Music 25
convicts 11, 20, 25
Coogee 17, 36, *122*
Cook, James 19, 20, 122
Coolangatta 46
Corbett Gardens, Bowral *148*
Corso, the 30, 37, *132*
Court House 44
Covent Garden Hotel *14*
Cowan Creek 18
Cowper Wharf Road 31
Cox
    Hill 47
    Philip 39, 72, 77
Craigieburn 44
Cremorne 29, 94, 97, *124–125*, 127
    Point 29, 127
Crescent Hill 41
Cronulla 35, 37
Cunningham, Dr Peter 13
Curl Curl Beach 38, *134*

Customs House *52*
Customs House,
    Newcastle 47

D

Darling
    Harbour 13, 17, 21, 23, 29, *38*, *39*, 68–69, *70*, *71*, *72*, *73*, *74–75*, 90
    Point 12, 30, 32, *107*, 109
    Ralph 39
Darlinghurst 31, 97, 100
    Road *30*, 31, *98*
Darwin, Charles 12, 17
Dawes
    Point 21, 22, 64
    Ridge 42
    William 42
Dee Why 38, *135*, 136
Dixon Street 13, 14, *39*, *76*
Dobroyd Head *15*
Domain, the 23, 25, 26, 30
Donohoe, 'Bold Jack' 12
Double Bay 30, 33, 97, *108*, 109
Doyles Restaurant 33, *113*
Druitt Street 33, 88
Drummoyne 40
Dutch Gable House *65*

E

Echo Point 42
elephants *18*
Elizabeth
    Bay House 31
    Farm *41*
    Street 34, 35, *79*
Empress Falls 43
Entrance, the 47
Eric Green reserve *138*
Essex Street 22
Evans Lookout *146*
Everglades 43

F

Fairfield 14
Fairy Bower Falls 45
Farm Cove 20, 25, 26, 29, *92*
Felix Bay *108*
Fern Tree Gully 45
ferries 21, *28*, 29, 30, *50–51*, *71*, *90*, 94, *95*
First Fleet 16, 20, 21, 25, 41, 53, 90
Fishermans Wharf, Watsons
    Bay 33, *113*
Fitzroy Falls 45, 46, *151*
Flagstaff Point *153*
Flemington 39
Florence Nightingale 24

Football Stadium 32
Fort
    Denison 29
    Scratchley 47
Freshwater 37, 38, 134, 135
funnel-web spider 19

G
galahs 19
Gap, the *115*
Garden
    Island *80*
    Palace Gates 25
Garigal Aboriginal Heritage
    Walk 18
Garrison Church 23, 40, 61
Gateway Plaza *86*
General Post Office 35
George Street 20, 22, 33,
    34, 39, *65, 66, 67,* 88
Gerringong 46
Gibson, Mel 36, 63
Gipps Street 32
Glebe 40, 97
Globe Street *66*
Gloucester Street 23
Glow Worm Glen 45
Gocher, William 37
gold rush 13, 85
Gosford 47, 145, 154
Government House 25
Grand
    Arch 43
    Canyon 45
    Synagogue 34
Greenbrier Park 44
Greenway, Francis 24, 25,
    27, 41, 114
Grose Valley *146*

H
Hacking River 18
Hampden Bridge *151*
Hampton Villa 40
Harbour
    Bridge 11, 21, 22, 23, *26,*
    27, 28, 29, 30, 39, 49,
    53, *56–57, 60, 61, 62,*
    63, 64, 90, *94*
    Tunnel 27
Harbourside
    Marketplace *13, 71*
    Station *73*
Hargrave, Lawrence 45
Harold Park Raceway 40
Harper's Mansion 44
Harrington Street 22, *64*
Harris Street 39
Harry's Cafe de Wheels 31
Hartley 43

Hawkesbury River 18, 24,
    41, 46, 141, 145, 154
Hay Street 14
Haymarket 14, 39, 97
Heron Cove *137*
Hogan, Paul 13, 26
Homebush Bay 38, 40, 97
Hornsby 46
Hughes, Robert 15, 41
Hungerford Hill 47
Hunter Valley 46, *47,* 145,
    156, 157
Hunters Hill 29, 40, 97
Hyde Park 12, 20, 25, 30,
    34, *78, 79, 80,* 105
    Barracks 24
Hydro-Majestic Hotel 43

I
Illawarra
    Escarpment 153
    Highway 44, 45
Inter-Continental Hotel 24

J
Jamberoo Valley 46
Jamison Valley 42, 43, 147
Jenolan Caves 43, *144*
Jervis Bay 46

K
Kahanamoku, Duke 37, *134*
Kanangra Walls 43
Kangaroo Valley *44,* 45, 46,
    145, 150, 151
kangaroos 18
Katoomba 43, *146,* 147
Kiama *45,* 46, 145
King Street 34, 87
King, Philip Gidley 16
Kings Cross *30, 31,* 32, 97,
    98, 99
Kirribilli *28,* 29
Koala Park Sanctuary 18, 97
koalas *18*
kookaburras 19
Ku-ring-gai Chase National
    Park 18, 19, 38, 46, 138,
    141, *142–143,* 145

L
La Perouse 17, *122, 123*
Lady Carrington Walk 17
Lady Martins Beach *108*
Laings Point 113
Lakes
    Budgewoi 47
    Macquarie 47
    Munmorah 47
Lang, Jack 27

Lavender Bay 27
Lawson 43
    William 42
Leichhardt 14
Les Girls 31
Leura 43
lifesaving 36, *37, 119*
Lion Island 18, 38, *140*
Little
    Bay 36
    Hartley 43
    Sirius Cove 29
Liverpool Street 32, 79
London Tavern *102*
Long
    Bay 36
    Reef 38, *136*
Lord Nelson, the 23
Lower Fort Street 61

M
Mabo decision 17
Macarthur, John 41
Mackenzies Point 119, *121*
Macquarie
    Elizabeth 23
    Lachlan 23, 24, 25, 27,
    34, 41, 47, 79
    Lighthouse *115*
    Pass 44, 45
    Place 24
    Street 24, 25, 26
    Watchtower *123*
Manly 18, 21, 28, 29, 30,
    35, 36, 37, 71, 94, 97,
    130–131, 132, 133
Mardi Gras 31, 97, *100, 101*
Market Street 33, 34, 35,
    81, 87, 88
Marks Park *121*
Maroubra 36
Martin Place 35, 87
Matraville 17
McRae, George 33
Megalong Valley 43
Middle
    Harbour *128, 129*
    Head 30
Milsons Point 26, 29, 61
Milton Park 44
Mining and Geological
    Museum *64*
Minnamurra 145
    Falls National Park 46
Mint Museum *85*
Mitchell
    David Scott 24
    Library *24*
Mittagong 44
Mona Vale 38, 137, 138

monorail 39, *72, 81*
Moore
    Alwyn 36
    Park 127
Mort, Thomas Sutcliffe 33
Morton National Park 45,
    151
Mosman 29, 94
    Bay 29, *124–125,* 127
Moss Vale 44, 45, 145, 151
Mount Wilson 15
Mrs Macquarie's Chair *23*
Mrs Macquarie's Point 23,
    25, 59, 61
Museum
    of Applied Arts and
    Sciences 85
    of Contemporary Art 21,
    29, 84

N
Nan Tien Temple *46*
National Maritime Museum
    39, *72, 73*
National Parks
    Blue Mountains *42, 146*
    Botany Bay *122,* 123
    Bouddi 47
    Brisbane Water 47
    Ku-ring-gai Chase 18, 19,
    38, 46, 138, 141,
    142–143, 145
    Minnamurra Falls 46
    Morton 45, 151
    Royal 17, 45, 145, *153*
    Sydney Harbour 16, 18,
    29, 30, 49, 109, *115*
    Wollemi 16
Neutral Bay 29, *124–125,*
    127
New South Head Road 32, 33
New South Wales Art Gallery
    28
Newcastle 27, 46, 47, 145
Newport 38
Newport Beach 137, *138*
Newtown *16*
Norman Lindsay Gallery and
    Museum 43
North Head 17, 49
Nowra 45, 46, 148

O
Olympic Games 15, 38, 40,
    41, 95, 97, 134
Opera House 11, 21, 22, 23,
    25, 26, 28, 29, *48,* 53,
    54–55, 56–57, 58, 59,
    60, 90, *94,* 95
Orient Hotel 22

Overseas Passenger Terminal 21, *52*
Oxford Street 30, 31, 32, 100, 104

P
Pacific Highway 46
Paddington 30, 31, 32, 40, *97, 102, 103,* 104
Paddy's Market 39
Palm Beach 35, 38
Park
    Hyatt Hotel *21, 22, 64*
    Street 79
Parliament House 24
Parramatta 21, 24, 29, 38, 40, 41, 94, 97
    River 23, 25, 28, 30, 40, 49, 94
parrots 19
Paterson, 'Banjo' 40
Pearl Beach 47
penal colony 19
Penrith 14
Peppers guesthouse *156*
Phillip, Arthur 11, 16, 19, 20, 21, 22, 25, 29, 46, 59, 90, 141
Pitcairn Island 63
Pitt Street 34, 35, *86, 87*
Pittwater 18, 38, *137,* 141
platypus 18
Playfair Street *65*
Point Piper 30, *108*
political refugees 15
Port Jackson 19, 20
Port Kembla 46, 153
Potts Point 31
Powerhouse Museum 31, 39, *85*
Premier's Office 24
Princes Highway 45, 145
Pymble 14
Pyrmont *38*, 40
    Bridge 39, *71, 72*

Q
Queen Victoria 24, 33, 35, 43, 88
    Building 33, *88, 89*
Queen's Square 24
Queenscliff *132*

R
Railway Square 39
rainbow lorikeets 19
Randwick Racecourse 32, *105*
Ranelagh House 45
real estate 12, 97

Redfern 17
    William 20
Regent Hotel 22
Reibey
    Mary 40
    Thomas 20
Reiby Place 20
Resch, Edmond 33
Richmond 12, 41
Riverside Park 44
Robertson 44, 45
Rock Baths *134*
Rocks, the 20, 21, 22, 23, 26, 40, 61, 63, 65, *66, 67*
Rose Bay 14, 29, 30, 33, *108, 110, 111*
rosellas 19
Roseville 14
Royal
    Botanic Gardens 20, 21, 24, *25,* 26, 29, 49, 61, *80, 92, 93*
    Hotel *103*
    Mint 24
    National Park 17, 45, 145, *153*
Rum
    Corps 22, 23
    Hospital 22, 24, 85
Rushcutters Bay 29, 32, *106*
Rydalmere Hospital 41

S
Sacred Heart Convent *111*
Sandringham Gardens *79*
satin bowerbird 19
Scenic Railway 43, *147*
Scotland Island 38
Seven Mile Beach 46
Shark Point *139*
sharks 19
Shellharbour 46
Shoalhaven River 45, 46
Skillion, the *155*
Skygarden retail centre *87*
Skyway 43
Smith's Creek 141, *142–143*
Smith, Charles Kingsford 46
South
    Coast 45, 148, 151, 153
    Head 49, 111, *114, 115*
Southern Highlands 44, 45, 46, 145, 148
Spit Bridge 18
Spit, the *128*
St Andrew's Cathedral 34
St James Road 79
St James' Church 25
St Mark's Church 32
St Mary's Cathedral 34, *83*

St Matthew's Anglican Church 41
St Scholastica's College 40
Stanwell Tops 45, 145, *153*
State
    Bank Centre 35
    Library of New South Wales *24*
    Theatre 35
Stockton 47
Strand Arcade *34*
Sublime Point 46
Suez Canal 22
Sunrise Point 45
Surf Life Saving Association of Australia 119
surfing *37,* 38
Surveyor General Inn 44
Susannah Place 23
Sussex Street 39
Sydney
    Aquarium 39, *70, 74–75*
    Art School 32
    Cove 21, 22, 25, 29, 41, *48,* 90, 91
    Cricket Ground *12,* 32
    Entertainment Centre 39
    Harbour *11,* 15, 16, 19, *20,* 23, 29, 30, 41, *56–57,* 63, *90,* 94, 95
    Harbour National Park 16, 18, 29, 30, 49, 109, *115*
    Hilton Hotel 34
    Hospital 22, 24
    International Aquatic Centre *40*
    Observatory *22,* 23
    Rowing Club 40
    Thomas Townshend 11, 20
    Tower 26, 35, *80, 81*
    Town Hall 20, *33,* 34
    University 28, 40, *83*

T
Tamarama 36, *120*
Tanna, Tommy 36
Taronga Park Zoo 17, 18, 21, 29, 94, *126, 127*
Taylor Square 31
Terrigal 47, *155*
Terry, Samuel 20
Thirroul 45
Three Sisters 42, *147*
Throsby Park 44
Treasury Building 24
Tropical Centre 26
Tudor House School 44
Tuggerah Lakes 47, *154*
Tumbalong Park 39
Turimetta Head 137

U
Ultimo 31, 38, 39, 97
Uniting Church 32
Utzon, Joern 28, 54

V
Vaucluse 33, *110,* 111
Vernon, W. L. 26
Victoria
    Barracks 32
    Park 40
    Street 31
vineyards 145, *157*

W
Wahroonga 17
wallabies 18
Walsh Bay 23, 61
Waratah Park 19
Wardell, William 34
Warriewood 38, *137*
Waterfront Restaurant *64*
Watson Road 23
Watsons Bay 29, 94, *112, 113*
Wentworth
    Falls 43
    William Charles 33, 42, 111
West Pennant Hills 18, 97
Western
    Distributor *38*
    Suburbs 35
Westpac Museum 65
Whale Beach 38, *139*
whipbird 19
White
    Australia Policy 13
    Patrick 12, 44, 104
Whiteley, Brett 45
William
    Square 30
    Street 31, 34, *98, 102*
Williams, Fred 36
Wilson, John 42
Windsor 41
Wollemi National Park 16
Wollongong 45, 46, 47, 145, 148, *152*
Woolloomooloo 30, *80*
    Bay 26, 31, *80*
    Gates 26
Woy Woy 47
Wyewurk 45

Y
Yester Grange 43
York Street 33, 88
Yacht Race, Sydney to Hobart *114*